MW01071679

Lucifer, Leviathan, Lilith, and Other Mysterious Creatures of the Bible

Joel R. Soza

Hamilton Books

An Imprint of
Rowman & Littlefield
Lanham • Boulder • New York • Toronto • Plymouth, UK

Copyright © 2017 by Hamilton Books
4501 Forbes Boulevard, Suite 200, Lanham, Maryland 20706
Hamilton Books Acquisitions Department (301) 459-3366

Unit A, Whitacre Mews, 26-34 Stannary Street,
London SE11 4AB, United Kingdom

All rights reserved
Printed in the United States of America
British Library Cataloguing in Publication Information Available

Library of Congress Control Number: 2017931006
ISBN: 978-0-7618-6897-2 (pbk : alk. paper)—ISBN: 978-0-7618-6898-9 (electronic)

∞™ The paper used in this publication meets the minimum requirements of American
National Standard for Information Sciences Permanence of Paper for Printed Library
Materials, ANSI/NISO Z39.48-1992.

Contents

Preface

This book is intended for a wide audience of readers. Its primary target is university and seminary students who are looking to enter into the theological thought world of the bible in a sophisticated way. However, scholars will also find it edifying, and intellectually rigorous lay persons of faith will find it stimulating, curios, and challenging. Professional clergy will advance their understanding of the thought world and theological message of the bible and will be more capable preachers, teachers, and expositors of the sacred text.

The study that is engaged in in this book is a theological pursuit of how, through one particular avenue of thought, the biblical writers framed the struggle of good and evil in the world. Through the use of imagination and playing off of common human apprehensions, their employment of creative imagery and portrayal of mysterious non-human beings brought out to the foreground in a resourceful way the taking on of some of humankind's other-worldly fears. Ultimately in the grand drama of scripture of course, these fears are put to rest by God's victory over all things evil through the kingdom of his messiah.

The bible's theological message is certainly diverse. The pursuit of this book is just one of many that could be undertaken, not only as relates to the overall theological message of the bible, but also as it relates to the specific topic of the struggle of good and evil and the mystery of the hidden world of spiritual darkness that exists in the biblical realm. To enter into this biblical realm requires great effort on the part of the bible reader to disengage pre-conceived notions of how the bible functions and to be prepared to engage a thought world that dates back millennia and crosses cultural and linguistic boundaries. Often times, a mistake is made when even a sophisticated biblical reader thinks of only having to cross linguistic lines when reading and studying the bible, rather than being aware that not only must language be translated, i.e. Hebrew, Aramaic, and Greek, but culture has to be translated as well. This can be the more challenging and urgent task. [1]

The book is organized around three main chapters. The first concerns "Lucifer," the second concerns "Leviathan," and the third concerns "Lilith." The ring of alliteration in the title is for remembrance purposes and to be catchy to create curiosity in would be readers. But the book is not just about, or even primarily about, Lucifer, Leviathan, and Lilith. Interwoven in these chapters is an exploration of other mysterious creatures that appear in the bible in an attempt to be as comprehensive as possible. The bible, whether one approaches it as a book of living faith, or merely as a historic exposition of ancient religion, can be a strange and mysterious world. This author does write from a faith perspective, and a Christian faith perspective at that, but it is the purpose of this book to tap into some of the mystery to be found in the pages of the bible as it relates to the various creatures that appear to be images of the struggle between God and the forces of chaos opposed to him. I hope you find the journey beneficial and intriguing.

NOTE

1. John H. Walton, *The Lost World of Genesis One* (Downers Grove, IL.: InterVarsity Press, 2009), pp.9-15.

Introduction

Some years ago I was participating in a conference for biblical scholars. The venue for the event was at a lodge in one of the state parks in Ohio. While doing some reading in my room, I noticed that there was literature laid about which was advertising another conference that was soon to be hosted at the lodge. The conference would be devoted to the topic of "Bigfoot," the legendary creature which roams the woodlands of North America. My interest was piqued, in that such fascination with the celebrated beast could lead to organized, formal, and even intellectual conferences that would draw paying participants. In considering the bible that I was studying in the moment, it occurred to me that the bible itself has its own fascinating world of the strange, mysterious, and mythical. This planted a seed which I am now seeking to water and nourish through the writing and publication of this book.

"Bigfoot," as the creature is called in the United States,[1] is the equivalent of Asia's Yeti, sometimes affectionately known as the "Abominable Snowman." I can recall childhood Christmas stories which featured this creature known as the "Abominable Snowman," never realizing until now that such a creature has its own storied history of supposedly roaming the Himalayas.[2] Perhaps the best known of all modern day mysterious creatures whose existence is in serious doubt is the water going Loch Ness monster, in which experts have estimated that there is one sighting for every 350 hours spent watching the Scottish lake.[3] What captures my attention is not the so-called sightings, but the amount of hours spent by people observing the lake for any signs of the aquatic animal. Although I've never been a believer, I must confess that if I had opportunity to be at or on the lake, my head would be turning in every direction to watch for "Nessie," as the monster is warmly known by locals. And it is this sort of thing that motivates me to pursue this topic in the writing of this book. What is it about us humans, even us modern day humans, living well beyond the enlightenment and the rise of the scientific age that causes us to be curious about the existence of creatures that most would write off as superstitions? And, how does the bible, written in antiquity when superstitions were much more prevalent, capture this human fascination by portraying its theological message at times with mysterious and even perhaps mythological beings?

It has become evident in the last century or so in the western part of the world that the frightening creature or monster business is indeed big business. The young 19th century English girl, Mary Wollstonecraft Shelley, could have never envisioned that when she first sat down to write the story of Frankenstein as a sort of competitive pleasure, that books, stage plays, and eventually movies about her creature would be the result of her efforts.[4] Prior to Frankenstein, there were other stories of feared creatures which preyed upon the imagination of the human mind. The tale of Dracula, made famous as a novel by Bram Stoker and as a film starring Bela Lugosi, dates much further back to earlier times, such as the Middle Ages, when especially in eastern Europe there was abounding folklore about blood sucking vampires who were responsible for sudden deaths, epidemics, plagues, and contagious disease.[5] Legends about vampires can be found in other parts of the world as well, for instance: Africa, Arabia, China, and India.[6] There are even records of vampirism in the annals of the ancient Babylonians and Assyrians,[7] and we shall see in our study that one of our mysterious biblical creatures is "Lilith," who has associations with being a night-roaming being who seeks the blood of children. Much is to be said of this in the main body of the book. The very name "Dracula" means "son of the devil" and captures the essence of how there is a perceived supernatural fight between God and the devil where, in the bible, the devil uses monstrous creatures as his cohorts and is himself such a creature in combat with God.[8] We might also add that Europe has been known for its tales of the werewolf as well. The werewolf has been a popular feature of movies since 1913.[9] These are just a few examples of society's fascination with monsters and mysterious creatures, and time would fail me to speak of the creature from the black lagoon, the mummy, the phantom of the opera, or mermaids and unicorns. The bible, written some two millennia or more ago is very insightful then, as to how it makes use of such creatures, real or imagined, to demonstrate the long-standing feud between chaos and order, or good and evil.

Returning momentarily to the topic of the present day public interest in "Nessie," one finds that she, as a monster of the waters, is predated by mariner's tales of long ago. The legendary Norwegian Sea monster known as the "Kraken" is one such example, as are the stories of deep sea creature encounters by New England mariners of the early 19th century. In fact, stories of watery monsters are to be found in the earliest human epics of the account of creation of the cosmos. The Mesopotamian creation epic Enuma Elish, which dates to the 12th century BCE and perhaps earlier, tells tales of the rebellious goddess Tiamat, who employs sea creatures and deities to carry out her work of theocide.[10] Tiamat even gave birth to a variety of bloodthirsty monsters, serpents, and dragons to rally them on her side against the opposing gods.[11] Even the bible's first recorded creation account, found in the opening chapter of the book of Genesis, speaks of God creating the "sea monsters" (Gen

1:21), a translation that is preserved in the American Standard and New American Standard Versions as well as the Revised Standard and New Revised Standard Versions. The theology behind the depiction of the God of Israel creating the sea monsters is to demonstrate that he is in control of these creatures. And, as we shall see by our study of the biblical water animal "Leviathan," such creatures are representative of humankind's worst fears and the mystery of evil and chaos in the world. The dragon like features of Leviathan is notable, seeing that "of all imaginary creatures, the dragon can be said most accurately to have universal appeal."[12] "The most ancient traditions about dragons go back to the Sumerian, Akkadian, and Egyptian mythologies of the first three millennia BCE."[13] Dragons, for the most part, "… represent forces or elements that interfere with the correct order or functioning of the world …"[14] They need to be conquered. The legend(s) of St. George in early Christian traditions slaying the dragon is symbolic of Christianity's view of its superiority to all things pagan and its victory over evil.[15] A similar example comes from the circa 8th century CE English heroic poem *Beowulf,* which tells of how the hero Beowulf courageously dispatches the dragon like monster Grendel, who ravaged the European landscape.[16] In a word, legends, stories, myths, and so forth of mysterious creatures and monster like beings are a part of the landscape of human culture and human history. Their purpose appears to be for more than mere entertainment, but probably represent something deep within the human psyche about numerous matters including the struggle of human life against the fears of things both seen and unseen to the human eye.[17]

"Human beings have always been mythmakers" is how Karen Armstrong begins her book *A Short History of Myth.*[18] This is evident even from the graves of Neanderthals she explains, who through their burial practices reveal a belief that beyond their mortality there was a counter-narrative of some sort that was a reality outside of the known material world.[19] It was a way to explain the working of the world and to deal with some of life's harshest realities. Such imagination is a characteristic of the human mind that does not exist elsewhere in the animal kingdom and helps humans to deal with the meaning of life and to agonize about the human condition in ways that, a dog for instance, does not upon the death of a fellow dog.[20] It takes a certain amount of human imagination to navigate life the ancients would have us believe, for even modern day scientists employ imagination to bring new knowledge to light and to forge ahead with new technologies.[21] The truth of myth is not in providing factual information, but in its effectiveness to give us new insight into the meaning of life.[22] It will be argued in the present work that the reader of the bible must be able to read with similar imagination in order to grasp the meaning of the bible in ways that the ancient writers intended. A flat and merely literalistic reading of the bible, especially in those parts where the genre demands more than just a straight forward reading, will render the reader void of understanding. Knowledge of mythology has at one time in the past even been considered "the hallmark of a person's education."[23] In fact, Armstrong who begins her book with "human beings have always been mythmakers" concludes her book with a strong challenge to religious leaders to be responsible in instructing in mythical lore when it comes to teaching from the bible.[24] If such religious teachers are incapable of doing so, the task will inevitably fall to others, such as artists and creative writers.[25]

In sum, the idea of myth as a literary category functions as a typology of a larger world not visible to the human eye.[26] In the words of David Adams Leeming

> As we explore the world of myth, we should remember that we are journeying not through a maze of falsehood but through a marvelous world of metaphor that breathes life into the essential human story: the story of the relationship between the known and the unknown, both around and within us, the story of the

search for identity in the context of the universal struggle between order and chaos.[27]

Alexander Eliot creatively and cleverly calls it "the myth dimension," in playing off of the abstraction in physics of that extra
dimension outside of spatial dimensions and the dimension of time
that is commonly referred to as "the 5th dimension."[28] The bible is
full of the mysterious, the strange, and the sometimes mythical. In
the present day there may be fascination with Bigfoot, Yeti, or the
Loch Ness Monster, but rigorous and imaginative readers of the
bible will want to enter into the world of mysterious creatures and
beings such as Lucifer, Leviathan, Lilith and others, trying to ascer-
tain the meaning behind these entities and the texts which discuss
them.

We will have a look therefore at the biblical texts which discuss
mysterious creatures. Our point of entry will be the Old Testament
book of Isaiah, for it is the only book of the bible to mention all
three of the primary creatures we will examine in our study: Lucifer, Leviathan, and Lilith. All three are mentioned just one time in
the text of Isaiah. "Lucifer" is found in 14:12, "Leviathan" is found
in 27:1, and "Lilith" is found in 34:14. Those familiar with critical
study of the book of Isaiah will recognize that all three of the verses
are found in the so-called "First Isaiah."[29] This increases the likeli-
hood of the same author or group of authors being responsible for
the mentioning of the three creatures in what is now sacred text for
Jews and Christians. So authorship issues will be minimized and
the assumption that the historic writer is the great prophet himself
is not far-fetched. The literary complexity of the modern day era
concerning the text and authorship of Isaiah proposed by Bernhard
Duhm and others has placed Isaiah into prominence as a biblical
book to be studied. However, not withstanding, Isaiah always held
a place of prominence in the canon anyhow because of such consid-
erations as its signal position at the head of the Latter Prophets, its
large size, its references in the New Testament, and its emphasis on

futurism, salvation, and the role of the Messiah. Ambrose is reported to have responded to the inquiring Augustine about which book of the bible should be studied first with the reply "Isaiah."[30]

We will not stay exclusively in Isaiah of course, but will explore a range of thought on our topic of mysterious creatures that might be found in the witness of Genesis to Revelation and some deutero and non-canonical literature is likely to make an appearance as well. Although being exhaustive is rarely a realization in the pursuit of any topic, we will try to leave as few stones unturned as is possible. The first chapter of the book studies "Lucifer," but will include an investigation into names and beings associated with him, such as Satan, the devil, and the world of angels and the demonic. Chapter two has a look at "Leviathan" and cognate topics such as serpents, sea monsters, Behemoth, Rahab, and dragons, beasts, and creatures of apocalyptic literature in the bible. The final chapter explores the phenomenon of "Lilith," in both the biblical and post-biblical world. We will then complete our study with some final reflections in the conclusion of the book. The intended result of reading this book is that one might be more fully engaged with an appreciation of the theological depth and breadth of the bible while grasping the tremendous significance of the imagery under discussion for understanding one's place in the world in the conflict between chaos and order.

NOTES

1. Also known as "Sasquatch" in Canada.

2. Macmillan Profiles Reference, *Myths and Legends* (New York, NY.: Macmillan Library Reference, 2000), p.41.

3. Angus Hall, *Monsters and Mythic Beasts* (Garden City, NY.: Doubleday and Company Inc., 1976), p.76.

4. Ibid., p.132.

5. Macmillan, *Myths and Legends*, p.341.

6. Ibid., p.340.

7. Malcolm South, *Mythical and Fabulous Creatures: A Sourcebook and Research Guide* (New York, NY.: Peter Bedrick Books, 1987), p.244.

8. Macmillan, *Myths and Legends*, p.343.

9. South, *Mythical and Fabulous Creatures*, p.265.

10. David Adams Leeming, *The World of Myth: an Anthology* (NY, Oxford: Oxford University Press, 1990), pp.18-23.

11. Kevin Osborn and Dana L. Burgess, *Classical Mythology: the Complete Idiot's Guide* (New York, NY.: Alpha Books, 1998), p.27.

12. South, *Mythical and Fabulous Creatures*, p.27.

13. Macmillan, *Myths and Legends*, p.71.

14. Ibid., p.71. Although conversely, in China, dragons can represent the embodiment of gentleness and goodwill. Hall, *Monsters and Mythic Beasts*, p.10.

15. Hall, *Monsters and Mythic Beasts*, p.8.

16. Donald B. DeYoung, *Dinosaurs and Creation: Questions and Answers* (Grand Rapids, MI.: Baker Books, 2000), p.44.

17. Hall, *Monsters and Mythic Beasts*, p.9.

18. Karen Armstrong, *A Short History of Myth* (Edinburgh, New York, Melbourne: Canongate, 2005), p.1.

19. Ibid., p.1.

20. Ibid., p.2.

21. Ibid., pp.2-3.

22. Ibid., p.10.

23. Osborn and Burgess, *Classical Mythology*, p.xxi.

24. Ibid., p.149.

25. Ibid., p.149.

26. Kenneth C. Davis, *Don't Know Much About Mythology* (New York, NY.: Harper Collins Publishers, 2005), p.24.

27. Leeming, *The World of Myth*, p.8.

28. Alexander Eliot, *The Global Myths: Exploring Primitive, Pagan, Sacred, and Scientific Mythologies* (New York, NY.: The Continuum Publishing Company, 1993), p.17.

29. Scholars have given the designation of 1st Isaiah to chs. 1-39 of the book, and 2nd and 3rd Isaiah to chs. 40-55 and 56-66 respectively.

30. Christopher R. Seitz, *Isaiah 1-39 (Interpretation: A Bible Commentary for Teaching and Preaching)* (Louisville, KY.: John Knox Press, 1993), p.1.

Chapter One

Lucifer

The being known as "Lucifer" is no stranger to the secular world. Many folks outside the Christian Church or Jewish Synagogue would immediately make some sort of association with the concept of the devil upon hearing of the name "Lucifer." There would also be considerable negative reaction that any belief in such a being is outmoded and might be considered a form of extremism advanced by those in the Church or other sacred culture. There is even a worldview called "Luciferianism" that has a kind of positive spin on Lucifer. It is not a specific dogma, but is rather a wide range of beliefs whose goal is enlightenment for personal growth and an ability to determine for oneself what is right and what is wrong.[1] The name was almost certainly selected for the worldview because the word Lucifer means "morning star," and is as such considered to be a symbol of enlightenment.

ISAIAH 14 & LUCIFER

In the bible Lucifer is known for a passage found in Isaiah 14, with a special interest in v.12, "How you are fallen from heaven, O Day Star, son of Dawn! How you are cut to the ground, you who laid the nations low" (NRSV)! Specifically, v. 12 uses the Hebrew word

הֵילֵל, which means "shining one" (translated here in the NRSV as "O Day Star"). This is the only place in the Old Testament where this word is found. In the Latin Vulgate translation, this Hebrew word was translated as "Lucifer" and was so translated in the 1611 King James edition of the English Bible as well as the late 20th century Living Bible. In brief, "Lucifer" is a Latin word that has survived and thrived because of especially the King James Version's preservation of the word in its English text.[2] It's meaning in English however can be seen in many of the other English translations, which translate הֵילֵל as something akin to "star of the morning" (e.g. New American Standard Bible, New International Version, Common English Bible, Contemporary English Version, and many others).[3]

Isaiah 14 may be categorized as a type of Old Testament prophetic speech commonly known as oracles against foreign nations that is employed not only in a large section of the book of Isaiah (chs.13-23), but in Jeremiah (chs.46-51), Ezekiel (chs.25-32), and is scattered around various books of the minor prophets as well. Its function is to demonstrate Yahweh's hegemony over the world and to provide Israel and Judah with the notion that there is a sense of righteous judgment outside of their own borders. Thus it was primarily a tool for encouragement to Yahweh's own people as much as it would have served as a warning to gentile nations. The passage in question about Lucifer, specifically Isa 14:4-23, is indeed just such an oracle against a foreign nation; in this case, it is Babylon that is targeted and has been since chapter 13. In fact, Babylon, somewhat surprisingly, is targeted first amongst a list of many, in that one might expect Assyria to head the list seeing that they are the primary nemesis to Israel/Judah during the days of the prophet Isaiah.[4] This taunt is specifically a funeral dirge for the king of Babylon, by which it may be argued that the king was alive at the time of the writing of the passage.[5] The list of suggested kings whom might be the intended audience is formative indeed and not a few scholars have spilt ink on the topic. However, John Oswalt, in his commentary on Isaiah rightly states, " . . . the attempt to identify a precise historical figure is probably futile . . . "[6] This passage is symbolic of any arrogance raised up against God, and to press for one intended subject probably misses this point. Nonetheless, whoever might be the identity of this so-called "morning star" (Lucifer), it is clear from the context that it refers to a king of Babylon who is human (v.16 "is this the *man* who made the earth tremble?"). So judging from the context and the plain reading of the text Lucifer is simply a name being given to some arrogant king of Babylon who stands for anyone who would attempt to supersede God. A possible irony here is that the background of the taunt might come from Babylonian stories and literature,[7] although there is no prototype for the הילל passage[8] and no such myth has been found amongst Canaanites or other peoples.[9]

EZEKIEL 28 & LUCIFER

The point of the taunt against this "Lucifer" is that human tyranny and oppression has now been removed from the earth when this Babylonian leader, or for that matter, any human dictator, has been removed, whether past, present, or future. But to get this point across, Goldingay argues that Isaiah has strategically used motifs from foreign myths that his audience would have been familiar with. The "morning star" language is likely to have come from titles of Canaanite deities.[10] A similar account can be found in Ezekiel 28:12-19, an incredibly poetic passage with Garden of Eden imagery that recounts the arrogance of a king of Tyre. As in Isaiah 14, so this too is in the context of oracles against foreign nations and is a similar taunt against the pride of human kings. The concern of these texts seem quite obviously to be directed towards the sin of human power players, and in fact, in the passage just preceding the king of Tyre passage, there is a message directed toward the ruler of Tyre where he is clearly identified as a man ("you are a man and not God," Ezek 28:2,9). As we shall discuss later in this chapter, these passages have taken on a life of their own regarding non-human entities in Christian theology. Although the origins of the passages are from ancient near eastern mythology, the question as to whether or not they have meaning beyond their original intended human target is yet for us to explore.

In Canaanite mythology there is a deity associated with the planet Venus.[11] Scholars understand the text of Isaiah to be borrowing from this mythology because Venus shines brightest at dawn just prior to being eclipsed by the rising sun every day, hence the phrase "son of the dawn" in Isa 14:12.Venus just suddenly descends without the completion of a true arc.[12] George Buchanan Gray points out that this "astral myth" could possibly be about the "waning crescent moon in the morning sky," or, if about the disappearance of Venus it could be more in seasonal terms rather than as concerns the planet's daily disappearance.[13] The theological connection to make is that human power brokers may ascend to prominence but are suddenly overshadowed by something greater than themselves, as the sun outshines other luminaries. This real or hypothetical king of Babylon is just a "star of the morning," i.e. a "Lucifer," to quote the Latin translation, whose moment of stardom comes and goes as he is brought down to earth and the reality of the lowly grave.

The difficulty in reading this one and only biblical "Lucifer" text (i.e. Isa 14:12) is knowing what to do with it now. Should it be left as a poetic passage using ancient mythical imagery that simply embellishes the point about the temporary nature of human power and the eventual fall and disgrace of human arrogance? Or does it somehow, in its association with "the banishment of a divine being from heaven,"[14] suggest that Christian theology is on track when it interprets Isa 14:12 as a reference to a literal angelic type being who once upon a time contended with God and was cast out of the heavens for an attempt at supercessionism? Christopher Seitz, in his commentary on the Isa 14 taunt against the Babylonian king chooses to not even mention the "Lucifer" translation and the corresponding Christian doctrinal claims about Lucifer as a proto-type of Satan. I can only guess that this is a purposeful move to demonstrate that many scholars such as himself might see the entire Lucifer doctrine as a grossly exaggerated and mis-guided interpretation of Isa 14:12. Therefore, according to him, it's not even worth mentioning. John D.W. Watts, in his commentary on the passage appears to also have a somewhat skeptical approach to Christian teaching on the literalism of such a supernatural being opposed to God, but rather than leaving it out of discussion, as Seitz does, he qualifies it. The passage, according to Watts, should be understood as a "Lucifer myth" that is a simile to picture the fall and disgrace of a tyrant.[15] If Christians are to use it as a reference to Satan, Watts would contend that our understanding of such an adversary to God should be left in the shadowy mythical background of the Isa 14 poem without taking the poem out of its context as an oracle against a Babylonian king.[16] Part of his argument is that Rev 12, a text which we shall look at later on, identifies the fall and defeat of one known as: dragon, serpent, devil, Satan (v.9), but makes no reference to Isa 14.[17]

There has been mixed opinion in Christian tradition regarding the interpretation of the "Lucifer" text. For instance, whereas some church fathers linked the passage to Luke 10:18 and Rev 12:8-9 regarding the fall of Satan, the reformers were unanimous in arguing that the context could support no such interpretation.[18] But because there was support in earliest Christian interpretive circles for linking the Isa 14:12 text with Satan, the term "Lucifer," which we have already established means "morning star," had eventually become the proper name of Satan. Later popular literature, such as Dante's *The Divine Comedy*,[19] demonstrates the kind of notoriety the name and person of Lucifer would carry. Why even the more recent Rolling Stones rock band made use of the name Lucifer in their popular song *Sympathy for the devil*.[20] The career of Lucifer has been rather spectacular when one recognizes that the term appears only once in the bible, and even at that, it is a Latin, not a Hebrew, Aramaic, or Greek word.

SATAN

Having made note of the origin and rarity of the word "Lucifer" in the bible let us move on to other biblical terms that are associated with the character that Lucifer came to be. "Satan" is probably the most obvious. The Hebrew word שׂטן simply means "adversary." This word is used in the Old Testament on a number of occasions, but, surprisingly, as an apparent other-worldly being, occurs in only two, maybe three places there. In the Hebrew Bible order of the canon, one would first come across the person of Satan in Zech 3:1, a text that is late in the Old Testament tradition. The context is the fourth night vision of the prophet Zechariah where Joshua the high priest is standing before the angel of the Lord in the divine council to be accused by another.[21] The accuser is "Satan" in the Hebrew text, but notably, the definite article appears before the word, thus literally "the Satan." In the Hebrew language the definite article cannot precede a proper noun;[22] just as in English one would not say "the George" or "the Sally." *The Jewish Study Bible* is careful not to translate as "Satan" here as is typically done in English translations completed by Christian or non-Jewish scholars. Instead, it opts for "the accuser," thereby leaving a bit of mystery and open possibility for the identity of this being. The word "Satan" is used twice in the Hebrew text of Zech 3:1, once as a noun for the actual being who is doing the accusing or opposing of the high priest, and once as a verb in an infinitive construct form to demonstrate what it is this being is doing. In short, the accuser is accusing.[23] The context of a divine vision which sees into the divine council with a mystery accuser and Joshua standing in the presence of God leaves this passage as somewhat enigmatic, much like the book of Zechariah itself. Jewish commentators would resist being too quick to link this story with this being that we have been discussing as "Lucifer," but would instead caution us to realize that in its Old Testament context "the Satan" here in Zech 3 could refer to any number of beings in God's royal heavenly court who are simply used for his purposes to test the faithfulness of God's people.[24]

Something similar can be seen in the opening chapters of the book of Job, the second occurrence in the Hebrew Bible of this other-worldly being known as "Satan." Here, this "adversary" is numbered with "the sons of God" and is referred to with the definite article fourteen times throughout Job 1-2.[25] Could this be a specific son of God that holds the office of an accuser, or might it be any unspecified member of the heavenly assembly acting as an adversary on behalf of God to challenge Job's faithfulness?[26] There is no doubt that this being is certainly a precursor to the later development of the devil, but at the time of the story of Job such associations were not present.[27] The development of the embodiment of evil being in one creature opposed to God is, like the monotheistic God himself, the result of a slow and evolutionary process with many twists and turns.[28] The annoying troublemaker of the Old Testament who is a lieutenant to God for his purposes is yet to become the full blown independent adversary of God to be seen in the New Testament. In the book of Job "The Satan" appears only in the first two chapters and then drops out of sight for the rest of the book. However, the appearance of Leviathan and Behemoth later on in the book might represent analogous adversity to Job, and thus the mysterious creatures in the book of Job: the Satan, Leviathan, and Behemoth, are all serving similar theological purposes as images of evil, chaos, and adversity. Leviathan and Behemoth are discussed in chapter two of this book.

The Zechariah and Job accounts of "the Satan" are similar in their noun construction (using the definite article) and in their portrayal of an adversary who has access to the presence of God and accuses God's people. There is another occurrence in the Old Testament of Satan as a possible other-worldly being.[29] It comes at the concluding books of the Tanakh and is very, very late in the tradition. This text, found in 1 Chron 21:1 tells of "Satan" arising against Israel and inciting King David to number the people of Israel. There is no definite article here. It is simply "an adversary" who influences David in this passage, and it could be as much human, possibly a military leader,[30] as it is supernatural. But the real curiosity is how the earlier parallel text, 2 Sam 24:1 tells the story. Here, it is Yahweh, the Lord himself who's anger burns against David and causes the inciting of David to carry out the census. Modern scholars have made attempts to harmonize the passages by combining the two texts and concluding that Yahweh used Satan as his instrument in carrying out the deed.[31] This is at least consistent with "the Satan's" activity in the book of Job. Wray and Mobley would contend that although the definite article is not here as it is in the Zechariah and Job texts, the term "Satan" in 1 Chron 21:1 should be understood as a proper noun anyhow. There is therefore, according to Wray and Mobley, a subtle change and "significant turning point"[32] taking place in that the underling of Yahweh is starting to act alone by this late place in the canonical Hebrew Bible. This adversarial being is no longer "the Satan" but is now just "Satan," which will set the table for his intrusive appearance in the New Testament. To quote Wray and Mobley further, "It is as if Satan is stepping away from the shadowy ranks of the heavenly host at the back of the stage, chanting their 'Holy, Holy, Holies,' to emerge front and center as a character in his own right. Satan – no longer God's lackey as in the book of Job – stands alone in Chronicles, acting apart from the divine council."[33]

This change in the later Chronicles text is indicative of how Jews in the late Old Testament period began to associate all evil with the person of Satan. For instance, the intertestamental work known as *Jubilees* has a Satan-like figure named "Mastema" who appears before God to challenge Abraham's good reputation with a request to have him offer up Isaac (Jub 17:15-18:19). The story clearly borrows imagery from the book of Job, stating, "And Prince Mastema came and he said before God, 'Behold, Abraham loves Isaac, his son. And he is more pleased with him than everything. Tell him to offer him (as) a burnt offering upon the altar. And you will see whether he will do this thing. And you will know whether he is faithful in everything in which you test him.'"[34] God responds in a manner similar to his response to the Satan in the book of Job, "And the Lord said, 'Speak to him. Do not let his hand descend upon the child. And do not let him do anything to him because I know that he is one who fears the Lord.'"[35]

In essence, *Jubilees*, a second century BCE work, has superimposed the Job story back upon the early Abraham story in an attempt to perhaps alleviate God from some of the responsibility for the terrible testing of Abraham in his request to have him sacrifice his son. A shameful accuser is instead responsible for instigating the binding of Isaac, just as "the Satan" is responsible for launching the misery of Job. Mastema therefore is an extra-biblical image of evil and is an extension of our Lucifer/Satan biblical characters. As in Job, so also then in Abraham the origin of evil is a mysterious being but the antidote in both cases is God. In fact, Mastema in *Jubilees* is also responsible for the strange attack on Moses because of his apparent lack of circumcision, a bizarre story recorded in Exod 4:24 (Jub 48:2-3). This acquits God of any perceived foul play. But toward the end of the book of *Jubilees* evil beings such as Mastema give way to Satan.[36] The same is the case for the intertestamental work known as *1 Enoch*, which dates roughly between 200-60 BCE.[37] The Qumran community responsible for the famous Dead Sea Scrolls understood the world to be dualistic, with Satan being an active force in charge of a legion of followers in combat with God. The *Damascus Covenant* within the Dead Sea Scrolls specifically mentions Satan and his involvement in this conflict: "During all those years Satan shall be unleashed against Israel."[38]

And then there are influences on the development of Satan that come from outside of Israel over a lengthy span of time and a lengthy span of geography. From as early as the Mesopotamian tale of the Gilgamesh Epic across time and space including Baal and Mot in Canaanite religion, to Isis and Osiris in Egyptian mythology, to the role of Hades in the worldview of the Greeks, these nations and cultures had their own explanations of evil and malevolent beings. Perhaps most notable is the teaching of Zarathustra of Persia around 600 BCE. Zarathustra taught monotheism and a clear dualism in which the one god, "Ahura Mazda," was not the author of evil. There was instead a malignant being called "Ahriman" ("fiendish spirit") from which all evil emanates. From the standpoint of biblical study this becomes fascinating because of the question of the possible influence of such Persian thinking upon the later Old Testament books of Zechariah, Job, and Chronicles which all feature "Satan" per our discussion above, and which can all be dated to the Persian period. It has been common across time and cultures for people to look at the world through a dualistic lens to provide answers to our most troubling and perplexing existential questions. There can be little doubt that "the religions of Mesopotamia, Canaan, Egypt, Persia, and Greece—Israel's closest neighbors—influenced the development of the idea of Satan in Jewish religion and added elements to his character."[39] We have yet however to discuss what this might mean for reading the bible from confessional and faith contexts regarding the reality of Satan as an adversary in one's life and as the author of chaos and disorder. This we shall get to eventually.

By the time of the first century BCE it is apparent that "Satan" had become the popular designation for the evil one in a Jewish worldview.[40] The person of Satan had indeed evolved from a low-level cosmic lackey in the Old Testament to an independently acting devil that is in charge of his own lackeys and has his own adversarial agenda.[41] Satan acquired articulation and definition outside of the murky world of the Old Testament during the intertestamental period. Imagine for a moment the Old Testament is providing snapshots of Satan's infancy when he is swallowed up by photos of larger group pictures of the heavenly court where the central focus was on another member of the family, and rightly so, that being God.[42] By the time of the New Testament Satan is standing alone in photos, taking "selfies" if you will.

THE DEVIL

We have learned that the development of the character of Satan takes shape during the intertestamental period as can be seen in the person of Mastema, and this is true for other intertestamental characters that we have not discussed, such as: Beelzebub, Belial, Azazel and Samael. We shall refer to these other characters in a bit. But by the time of the New Testament "Satan" in particular as a proper name for the archenemy of God comes into perspective in ways that did not take place in the Old Testament. More than half of the some fifty occurrences of the word "Satan" in the bible show up in the much shorter New Testament.[43] He is a character that comes more to the foreground than what has been seen in reading just the Old Testament. Often times in the New Testament the synonym "devil" is used as well for Satan.[44] This can be seen for example in Rev 12:9, where Satan is not only the devil, but a serpent and dragon also. This apocalyptic verse is an important text, and we shall examine it momentarily. The word "devil," which in Greek is διάβολος, occurs thirty-eight times in the New Testament but is also to be found in the Septuagint, and in that Greek text, is the translation for שָׂטָן in Zech 3:1-3, Job 1-2, and 1 Chron 21:1. Its related verb means "to throw across," and thus reinforces the notion of Satan as an adversary who is trying to cause one to stumble in his opposition. For instance, the Old Testament story of Balaam and the talking donkey uses the word שׂטן in the Masoretic Text of Num 22:22 whereas the Septuagint uses the word διάβολος, both in reference to the "angel of the Lord" standing in the way of Balaam and the donkey as an enemy. One might not normally think of the angel of the Lord acting as a "satan" or "devil" but that is exactly what is happening in the Balaam story. This heavenly being is acting in a way which points to the literalness of the meaning of satan, which is that one is intentionally getting in the way to impede another's progress.

THE DEVIL IN THE SYNOPTIC GOSPELS

In regard to the New Testament synoptic gospels we are first introduced to Satan or the devil in the classic temptation in the wilderness story (Matt 4:1-11, Mark 1:12-13, Luke 4:1-13). The evangelists reveal that underneath the good news of the ministry of Jesus there is a tension between God and the forces of evil led by Satan.[45] Mark, traditionally thought of as the first written gospel, is borrowing from apocalyptic literature in that his brief account of the temptation in the wilderness is highlighted by how it is the "Spirit" who leads Jesus into the place of temptation.[46] There is a larger cosmic conflict here. The same could be said of Matthew and Luke's accounts, who also mention the Spirit in their expanded telling of the story. The more earthly conflict between Jesus and religious leaders such as the Pharisees that would soon be revealed could be said to simply be a reflection of this conflict and therefore the Pharisees are the pawns of the devil according to the evangelists' presentations. Matthew, presumably being written a decade or so after Mark would have other concerns as well, such as the aftermath of the devastation of the 1st century Roman-Jewish war and the resulting bewildered context of the Matthaen community.[47] For Matthew, the devil has been involved in the historic tragedy. Luke perhaps sees the devil as opportunistic and even more sinister than how Matthew and Mark describe him, as can be seen for instance in his claiming that the devil would wait for "an opportune time" following his failed attempt to get Jesus to take the bait in his 3-fold temptation (Luke 4:13). For Luke, it is Satan who has bound a woman with illness for eighteen years (Luke 13:16), which is perhaps a subtle hint that it is really the stubborn synagogue official who is bound by Satan in his ideology by not wishing the woman a healing on the Sabbath. Also for Luke, it is Satan who wishes to "sift Simon like wheat" at the Last Supper (Luke 22:31). It is a Satan similar to Job's Satan who demands to serve a testing function against the righteous, which is certainly what the initial temptation in the wilderness is about. Both Matthew and Luke record that in the temptation event Satan asserts that he is appointed to rule the kingdoms of the world. But it is only in Luke where Jesus claims that Satan's power will come to an end and that he was watching him "fall from heaven like lightning" (Luke 10:18).

There are two places in the three synoptic gospels where Satan or the devil is similarly referenced. One of these is the so-called parable of the sower and seed, also known as the parable of the four soils (Matt 13:1-9, Mark 4:1-9, Luke 8:4-8). In the subsequent interpretation which Jesus provides the Matthew account calls him "the evil one," the Mark account calls him by the proper name "Satan," and the Luke account goes with "the devil." It is evident in this parable that the proclamation of the word of the kingdom of Christ is actively opposed by this adversary who is trying to undo what the word does by attempting to steal it away. The other place in the synoptic gospels where all three evangelists tell a story involving the devil is the temptation in the wilderness that we have been discussing. In the Matthew and Luke telling of the story the adversary is called "the devil" continuously until, unique to Matthew's account, Jesus himself calls him out as "Satan" (Matt 4:10). This may be a way for Jesus to connect his tempter back to Job's experience where the well-known adversary there is literally "the satan." This would show Jesus to be righteous as Job was. It is not surprising to see Satan in this role again, for that is how we have primarily known him from the Old Testament. However, he seems to be acting more independently now, and the fuller story of Jesus right through the passion narrative will reveal the expanded role and activities of this devil. Luke leaves out the "begone Satan" words that Matthew has put in the mouth of Jesus. Mark's very short account never uses the term "devil" at all like Matthew and Luke, but rather briefly tells the story without any words of Jesus and the narrator calls the tempter "Satan." In Mark's two verse account (Mark 1:12-13) the ordeal must be a part of God's divine plan where God is yet in control of Satan because the encounter is framed in a way to show that it is "the Spirit" (v.12) who impels Jesus into the wilderness to be tempted by "Satan" (v.13) in a way that remembers the forty years of wilderness testing in the days of Moses. Matthew and Luke have also begun their temptation narratives with references to the Spirit, but Mark's account, as is typical of his style, is punctiliar, thereby highlighting the larger cosmic battle that is going on here between Jesus and Satan. It is from this first encounter with Satan in the New Testament and its representation of evil and chaos fighting against God that we have the notion of one being able to "sell their soul to the devil." This was not an option for Job, as he was unaware of how he was a pawn in a much larger cosmic conflict. But for Jesus, he could have accepted the devil's offer to have the kingdoms of the world in exchange for devil worship. He of course resisted and set an example for all later to follow in his rejection of the devil's claims and offers.

There are also two occasions where two of the three synoptic gospels refer to Satan. One involves Matthew and Mark and is the well-known and important incident often termed Peter's confession of the Christ (Matt 16:13-23, Mark 8:27-33). After an initial correct answer on the part of Peter in claiming Jesus as the Christ, he puts his foot in his mouth, as he is reputed to often do, by trying to forbid Jesus from going to Jerusalem to carry out his mission. The famous reply of Jesus, "get behind me Satan," is the immediate response. It seems most proper to interpret this, not as Peter being possessed by the devil, but rather that Peter is acting in a way that is typical of Satan. That is, he is attempting to block Jesus from obedience to God. Here then is the meaning of Satan in its most basic form.[48] Peter is not literally the devil in this moment, but he is acting adversarily to Jesus without even knowing it and is therefore being what the devil is, an enemy who is in opposition. Just as the angel of the Lord was a "satan" to Balaam and the donkey in Num 22:22 in a righteous way, so also Peter, in a not so righteous way, is a "satan" to Jesus on this occasion. It is a figure of speech. The other occasion of two of the three synoptic gospels referring to Satan is in Matt 12:22-29 and Luke 11:14-22. Jesus defends himself as not being Satan in his ability to cast out Satan for even the devil is smart enough to not destroy his kingdom in this manner. What is striking about the teaching of Jesus here is that as much as he is representing "the kingdom of God," so also Satan has his own kingdom ("how then shall his kingdom stand?" Matt 12:26, Luke 11:18). By this point in the bible the Satan that was a lesser known being in the royal heavenly court used by God as an adversary against Job now has his own kingdom. Things have changed and the stakes are higher than they ever were.

THE DEVIL IN THE FOURTH GOSPEL

Although we have been discussing a sort of evolution of Satan from background character in the Old Testament who comes to the forefront and into his own in the New Testament, the fourth gospel, the Gospel of John, characterizes the devil as having been involved since the first humans were alive, thus predating the activity of the devil in Job. It is recorded in John that Jesus said to the Jews, "You are of your father, the devil . . . he was a murderer from the beginning" (John 8:44), a reference to Cain's killing of Abel which is reinforced in 1 John 3 ("the devil has sinned from the beginning," v.8 and "not as Cain, who was of the evil one," v.12). A characteristic of the Gospel of John is that "John's Satan only appears in the forms of his human agents."[49] It is as it were, the devil incarnate, antitheses to Jesus as the Christ. Satan appears in the Gospel of John in the guise of people and organized religion and not so much as a freestanding supernatural being.[50] For instance, it is not the devil who is tempting Jesus to take for himself the kingdoms of the world as in the wilderness temptation, but it is instead the people who try to make him king, something Jesus resists (John 6:15). Instead of the devil trying to tempt Jesus into turning stones into bread, it is the people who ask for a supernatural sign related to bread (John 6:30-31). It is Jesus' own brothers who attempt to provoke him to display his powers in a public manner (John 7:1-5), reminiscent of the devil's wilderness temptation to do this with both the bread and jumping from the temple. And Judas is called "a devil" by Jesus (John 6:70) and in his betrayal of Jesus Satan "entered into him" (John 13:27). The battle on earth between Jesus and human agents is reflective of the cosmic battle taking place between light and darkness and good and evil, of which Jesus is the cosmic redeemer. John's Satan in the post Roman-Jewish war community is similar to the enemy that the Essenes dealt with and their juxtaposition of the "sons of darkness" and the "sons of light." And this work of Satan which according to John dates back to the time of the first family continues on beyond the passion and resurrection of Jesus and into the age of the church. In the book of Acts Satan continues to operate through people, filling the hearts of sinners (Acts 5:3) and blinding the Gentiles from being able to understand the Gospel (Acts 26:18).

THE DEVIL IN PAUL'S WRITINGS

We have thus far been tracing the development of the person of Satan across the Old Testament and from cultural influences outside Israel, along with the development of Satan in the intertestamental period and the Gospels and Acts of the New Testament. Things have been fairly straightforward in this evolution of the diabolical one. However, we now engage the Pauline corpus of literature in the New Testament and in doing so discover a Satan who is referred to fairly often and who seems to be wearing many hats. Paul speaks specifically of Satan some ten times, while also making reference to the term devil and related supernatural, evil powers on a number of occasions as well. His reference to Satan as an entity opposed to God is found in his Corinthian correspondence, letters to the Church at Thessalonica and to Timothy, as well as one passing and concluding reference in his letter to the Roman Christians.

A good place to start would be 2 Cor 12:7, where it is recorded by Paul " . . . there was given to me a thorn in the flesh, a messenger of Satan to buffet me . . . " (NASB). Paul clearly understood that he had an adversary in the traditional Old Testament sense hindering him to some degree. The English word "buffet" in the KJV and NASB of 2 Cor 12:7 come from the Greek verb κολαφίζω, which has strong connotations to being literally physically struck, as if with a fist. This is the term that is used to describe Jesus being slapped and beaten at his trial (Matt 26:67, Mark 14:65). Keep in mind that the satan in the book of Job was initially disallowed by God to touch Job, " . . . do not put forth your hand on him . . . " (Job 1:12). But after Job passes this first test the satan challenges God to "put forth thy hand, now, and touch his bone and his flesh . . . " (Job 2:5). When God states to the satan, "Behold, he is in your hand, only spare his life," liberty has now been given to the satan to attack Job's physical body, which is precisely what happens in the continuing narrative. Paul is in a sense then, like

Job, who is being physically attacked by Satan in his 2 Cor 12:7 description. It was being allowed by God. There has been lengthy debate as to the exact nature of this messenger from Satan and the affliction Paul faced, but most discussions have revolved around physical affliction. Some suggested interpretations are that Paul suffered from epilepsy, hysteria, depression, headaches, eye-trouble, malaria, leprosy, or a speech impediment. [51]

A similar, yet different kind of satanic hindrance against Paul and his mission can be seen in his correspondence to the Christians at Thessalonica. He writes, "For we wanted to come to you—I, Paul, more than once—and yet Satan thwarted us" (1 Thess 2:18). A different Greek word is used here for buffeting or getting in the way from the one we have seen in 2 Cor 12:7. It is the aorist active indicative of ἐγκόπτω, so that Satan's "thwarting" in this context is not with fist a cuffs so much, as it is blocking the way. This of course has strong association with what we have seen of satan in the Old Testament, illustrated for instance in the Balaam and donkey story where the angel of the Lord was acting as an adversary. The Greek word used in 1 Thess 2:18 is a term which was "originally used of breaking up a road to render it impassable and later it was used in a military sense of making a break through the enemy's line. It was also used in the athletic sense of cutting in on someone during a race. The general meaning of the word is 'to hinder'."[52] Paul uses it when he writes to the Galatian churches and chastises them for being "hindered" (Gal 5:7). He says the Galatians were "running well" but were now "hindered," and makes a subtle, but strong suggestion that it may have been Satan himself who was causing this hindrance, "You were running well; who hindered you from obeying the truth? This persuasion did not come from him who calls you" (Gal 5:7-8). Of course the larger context of the letter to the Galatians demonstrates that it is Judaizers who are the ones impeding the progress of the new Christians in the Galatian region. Paul has probably implied that it was such organized religion that was the satanic force here, thereby advancing the kind of thought we have seen in the Gospel of John, where for him and his telling of the Jesus story, people are the provocateurs of satanic work.

This Johannine theme of people as instruments of Satan is a Pauline theme as well. Besides that which we have already mentioned, people as satanic hindrances to the work of God can be seen in Paul's letters to the Corinthians, the Romans, the Thessalonians, and to Timothy. When Paul says to the Corinthians that Satan "disguises himself as an angel of light," (2 Cor 11:14) he is most obviously making reference to those false or super apostles whom he has been contending with in the Corinthian correspondence. The servants of Satan can "disguise themselves as servants of righteousness" (2 Cor 11:15). This is consistent with how Jesus called out certain Jews as recorded in the gospel of John as being of their father, who is identified as the devil (John 8:44). There may even be a faint hint here of Satan as having once been an "angel of light" according to the Lucifer tradition of Isa14, although the Corinthian context most likely does not allow for this being the case. When Paul concludes his letter to the Romans he tells them "the God of peace will soon crush Satan under your feet" (Rom 16:20) but does so in the context of having just warned them of "those who cause dissensions and hindrances" (Rom 16:17), which is characteristic of the meaning of Satan early on in the Old Testament as adversarial. In Paul's first letter to Timothy he speaks of younger widows who have "turned aside to follow Satan" (1 Tim 5:15). He no doubt does not mean that these young ladies have purposely, consciously, and with intentionality, made a deliberate choice to be Satan followers, but that their conduct and course of action is indeed after the pattern of Satan and have therefore become unwitting followers of the evil one. Once again, for Paul, people are used of Satan in ways that may be less than obvious to the undiscerning eye. When he speaks of "the man of lawlessness" in 2 Thess 2 he may have in mind the epitome of a human as an agent of Satan, for this is "the one whose coming is in accord with the activity of Satan" (2 Thess 2:9). But all that this man does is deception and delusion (2 Thess 2:10-11).

But for Paul, Satan has other roles besides just using people as hindrances to the work of God. He is a schemer, a punisher, and a tempter as well. In 2 Cor 2:11 Satan schemes a plot of unforgiveness amongst the Christians. He also is a punisher of some sort according to Paul, for the apostle was prepared to hand over to Satan sinners and blasphemers such as the sexually immoral man of the Corinthian church (1 Cor 5:5) and Hymenaeus and Alexander for their apostasy (1 Tim 1:20). Paul does not elaborate on just what exactly he means by "handing over to Satan," but according to Henry Kelly he is acting as some sort of police chief or disciplinarian.[53] And Satan is apparently one who tempts toward sin as well. In 1 Cor 7:5 Paul warns husbands and wives to fulfill their marital duties one to another so that Satan does not tempt because of lack of control in sexual matters. Paul was well acquainted with the vast literature of his tradition beyond the Hebrew Bible and may have been influenced by the sexual misconduct of extra-terrestrial beings that are spoken of in some of this literature. For instance, there is a story in *1 Enoch*, a book briefly alluded to earlier, of the "Watchers," angelic beings whose task it was to watch over the universe but instead mate with human women.[54] A similar story is told in *Jubilees*, where angels have intercourse with females of the human family resulting in a race of giants that beget murderous offspring.[55] These stories from such pseudepigrapha are without question elaborations of the strange tale told early in the sixth chapter of the book of Genesis regarding the Nephilim who are a product of the illicit union between the sons of God and the daughters of men. Behind the plot to corrupt the human race by violating sexual taboos is a Watcher named "Semyaz" who also goes by the names Semyaza, Semjaza, and Semihaza. To complicate matters more, this leader of disgraced angels is to be associated with the Mastema of the book of *Jubilees* that we have already spoken of, another fallen angel by the name of Azazel acting as a lieutenant, and lastly, by the end of the book of *1 Enoch* (37-71), Satan himself. There are therefore numerous disgraced angelic type beings in the two works known as *Enoch* and *Jubilees*, but what they share in common is the fact that by the latter portion of their respective books the trouble-maker and author of all things evil is known as "Satan." Returning back to Paul's knowledge of Satan and his warning to Christian married couples in 1 Cor 7:5 to protect that sacred sexual trust, this entire background of taboo sexuality on the part of the lust-filled angels may have been in mind. Satan tempts, and sexual sin is a high priority for him.

As far as Paul's use of the word "devil" (διάβολος) as a synonym for Satan, he employs it eight of the thirty seven times it is used in the New Testament. Interestingly, of the eight times he employs it he uses the term on three occasions to refer to humans acting in a diabolic way. He is the only New Testament writer to use the word with humans as the subject. That is, he charges people with doing that what we know the satan to have done in our earliest biblical recollections of him in Zechariah and Job—they are accusers, slanderers, or gossips. To narrow things down even more, Paul's three uses of the term διάβολος in this manner are only found in his pastoral epistles and is used once against older women (Titus 2:3), once against women in leadership (1 Tim 3:11), and once against humankind in general (2 Tim 3:3). He has a vested interest in preparing his younger ministry colleagues to be prepared to do battle against the diabolical ways of humans as much as the evil one himself.

THE DEVIL IN THE APOCALYPSE

However, the fullest account of Satan in the bible comes, not from the gospels or the Pauline corpus, but from the last book in the canon—the Apocalypse.[56] To quote Wray and Mobley on the matter,

> Every Satan we have seen to this point—whether it be those cancerous cells in the body of Christ that Paul demonizes, the Satan who appears in embodied form to do solo combat with Jesus in the desert or the evil spirit who enters persons like Judas—will appear in Revelation. In Revelation, Satan is a culmination of his many roles in earlier biblical, apocryphal, and pseudepigraphical texts.[57]

Satan is mentioned eight times in the book of Revelation. Five of these eight times he is referred to in John's letters to the seven churches of Asia in the early part of the Apocalypse. On the first (Rev 2:9) and last (Rev 3:9) of these occasions the "synagogue of Satan" is mentioned. The respective targeted churches are the churches at Smyrna and Philadelphia, cities which had Jewish populations to which John alludes. This Satan is a Satan consistent with what we have seen in the gospel of John as well as in Paul's writings; a Satan guised using people and false religion. To the church at Smyrna there is a switching of nouns from "Satan" to the "devil" in Rev 2:10, a devil who will cast some of the Christians into prison for a time of testing and tribulation. This prison is not further defined, but it is the first time we see the devil acting as a sort of jail keeper, a theme that will be popularized during the Christian ages regarding Satan living in Hell as the warden of damned souls. In Rev 2:10 however, the meaning appears more to be about the metaphorical prison of testing, trial, and tribulation. The anti-synagogue theme showing up in the correspondence to the churches of Asia is accompanied by another anti-establishment theme, namely a critique of Rome, both the Empire and the Emperor. This can be seen in the letter to Pergamum where "Satan's throne" (Rev 2:13) is mentioned and then is spoken of again in the same verse using the language of "where Satan dwells." The other place where Satan is referred to in the letters to the churches of Asia is in Rev 2:24 regarding Jesus' message to the church at Thyatira. The teaching of Jezebel is the topic of conversation and it is likely that this is more satanic work originating within false religion, probably once again, that of the Jews. Jesus calls this false teaching "the deep things of Satan."

After the introductory epistles to the seven churches of Asia where Satan has been named five of the eight times in the book of Revelation there is a gap until we see the term "Satan" mentioned again. We do not see him again until Rev 12:9. When we do, he is not just "Satan" but is also called in the same verse: "the great dragon," "the serpent of old," and "the devil." This, according to Wray and Mobley, is "the Satan we know and loathe, the cosmic opponent of God."[58] Another gap follows in the Revelation text, and we do not see the word "Satan" again until Rev 20:2 where the same exact description of "dragon, serpent, and devil" appears as in Rev 12:9. This double description of Satan with three other titles will be of special interest to us as we investigate the Leviathan creature in the second chapter of this book. For now, we will be content to note that Satan is bound for one thousand years (Rev 20:2) but is eventually released from his prison for a time (Rev 20:7). This is the last mention of Satan in the bible, although we know that he himself is thrown into the lake of fire as "the devil" to end his story once and for all (Rev 20:10). There is an interesting progression to note regarding Satan from his earliest days in the book of Job as one who seemingly has access to God and is one of his servants, to the Satan who by the end of the biblical story in the Apocalypse has been kicked out altogether and has no place any longer near God or humans but is "tormented day and night forever and ever" (Rev 20:10). In the in between Satan started to wear some of the hats that Saint Paul spoke of in his epistles as his role enlarged and as he began to have his own kingdom with minions and lackeys and all. He is even shown a bit of respect in the way that Michael the archangel will not "bring a slanderous accusation against him" (Jude 9, NIV), a text that Jude writes most likely taken from a pseudepigraphal literary work.[59] Michael refuses to be an accuser, the very thing that defines Satan. But in the Apocalypse Michael is no longer waging war with politeness and respect as he is engaged in cosmic combat with this ultimate enemy of God (Rev 12:7).

BIOGRAPHY OF THE DEVIL

In sum, we see that a biblical biography of Satan reveals that he emerges from the murky world of the Old Testament as the adversary and accuser that his name means. This is especially true in late texts such as Job 1-2, Zech 3, and perhaps 1 Chron 21:1. The development of Satan was no doubt influenced by foreign cultures of the ancient world such as Egypt, Mesopotamia, and Canaan, and by the time of the intertestamental period he is coming into his own in Jewish literature as an independent entity opposed to God and going by a variety of names and titles. In the New Testament Satan is in direct conflict with Jesus and acts as the tempter and accuser that he has shown himself to be in the Old Testament. Saint Paul refers to him a number of times in his writings and credits him with being not just the tempter and accuser, but one who plots schemes and can act as an instrument of punishment on behalf of God. He is the devil that Christians are at war with. This biblical biography reveals the devil's resume as one who was once upon a time a celestial functionary with freedom and limits who goes rogue, but whose rule will come to an end one day in a rather violent way. Nonetheless, popular understanding of the history of Satan is that he was once upon a time a good angel, Lucifer if you will, who was kicked out of heaven at some point and was involved with the temptation of Eve, perhaps because of jealousy over the newly created humans. He then goes on to continue to be a tempter and accuser of humans as well as some sort of jail keeper and tormentor of those souls who are lost in hell.

This popular understanding of Satan has been termed the "New Biography of Satan" by Henry Ansgar Kelly.[60] He argues for a return to what he calls the "Original Biography of Satan."[61] The primary difference between the two is the applying of the Lucifer myth in Isa14 to Satan, something that Kelly would argue is the consequence of the Church Father Origen's misapplication of this biblical text.[62] Kelly indeed calls it a "hijacking" and is adamant for a return to a biblical understanding of the biography of Satan.[63] He casts Origen's interpretive move in more recent Hegelian terms, claiming an original "dark thesis" about Satan that Origen counters with a "light antithesis" regarding Satan as having originally been an angel of light. Therefore, Satan must have fallen from heaven and Isa14 must be the biblical support for this. This resulted in a "light to dark thesis" that has now become popularized as the true biography of Satan.[64]

So, did Satan fall from heaven? One curiosity about this is that in the book of Job he apparently has freedom to come and go as he pleases in what would seem to be from the context, the heavenly realm.[65] This does not look like a Satan who has been cast out of the presence of God. But it is time to investigate Matt 11:20-24 and especially Luke 10:18 with the surrounding verses, because it has something to say about Satan falling from heaven. Hypothetically, both of these passages borrow from Q, the supposed common source to Matthew and Luke which has been lost to history as far as a surviving manuscript goes.

Matthew does not record Jesus as having said "I saw Satan fall from heaven like lightning" as Luke does (Luke 10:18). But he does seem to have Jesus referring to the two prophetic texts we spoke of earlier regarding the Lucifer myth: Isa 14 and Ezek 28. The context is Jesus' chastisement of the three northern Galilean cities where he conducted a majority of his ministry. Chorazin and Bethsaida are indicted for their failure to repent even though they had witnessed the works of power that Jesus had performed in those towns. They are compared to Tyre and Sidon, cities known for evils of their own, and yet these two cities would have responded much more favorably to the ministry of Jesus than Chorazin and Bethsaida. But it is Capernaum which takes the brunt of the woe oracle of Jesus. This city had basically been the center of Jesus' public ministry. He taught in their synagogue, cast out spirits in front of their eyes, healed Peter's mother-in-law, for this was Peter's very home town, and he healed the paralytic man who had been lowered through the roof. Jesus captures the language of Isa14:13&15 by saying of Capernaum that it will not "be exalted to heaven" but will instead "descend to hades" (Matt 11:23). In other words, Capernaum is a Lucifer that will have its brief morning star rise, but will in like manner suddenly fall as the king of Babylon. Jesus seems to have the Ezek 28 passage in mind as well during his critique of the Galilean cities when he likens Chorazin and Bethsaida to Tyre and Sidon, cities which are condemned one after the other in Ezekiel's oracles against foreign nations in the larger section of Ezek 25-32. Specifically, judgment on Tyre begins at Ezek 26 and continues through Ezek 28:19 before turning attention to judgment on Sidon in a much shorter section (Ezek 28:20-24). In fact, Ezekiel uses similar language to Isaiah's mentioning of a descent to hades in both Ezek 28:8 ("they will bring you down to the pit") and Ezek 28:17 ("I cast you to the ground"). To cast insult to injury, Jesus goes on to say about Capernaum, that basically Sodom, the city of absolute worse infamy and reputation, will be able to tolerate a day of judgment better than Capernaum.

When we look at the parallel passage in Luke regarding the denounced three Galilean cities we find a richer account because of the surrounding context. The denunciation is bordered by Jesus' sending out of the seventy disciples for ministry (Luke 10:1-11) and then receiving them back (Luke 10:17-20). We find therefore, words similar to the account in Matt 11 in the in-between section of Luke 10:12-16. There are a few subtle differences, but none of which would be worth diverting attention. The same Lucifer like dynamics is at work here. However, it is what Jesus says to the returning disciples that gives an interesting spin on things different from the Matthaen account. The disciples are ecstatic that their evangelistic mission has proved that the demons were subject to them in the name of Jesus (Luke 10:17) to which Jesus replies "I was watching Satan fall from heaven like lightning" (Luke 10:18). The interpretive complexity of Jesus' response is knowing how to locate what he means by this observation of Satan's fall. Is this a past tense occurrence referring to antiquity that would rightly place Satan as a greater fulfillment of the Lucifer passage in Isa 14:12? That is, Jesus in his pre-incarnate state witnessed the supposed kicking out of heaven of this adversary of old. Or, should it be understood as a present occurrence and a result of what was happening during the seventy disciples' mission? The latter choice seems likely and commentators would seem to support this interpretation more so. Some might even like the option of Jesus speaking about a future and apocalyptic Satanic falling from heaven in the manner of Rev 12. It is not perfectly clear then on how to interpret Luke 10:18 although one might be a bit more lenient than Kelly is on the Church father Origen, especially because resonances of both Isa 14 and Ezek 28 are in the immediate vicinity of Luke 10:18 which speaks of Satan's fall. But it is also worth reflecting upon the teaching of Jesus in what follows Luke 10:18. The "serpents, scorpions, and power of the enemy" (Luke 10:19) provides the sort of images of evil that is the larger concern of this book, and it is noteworthy that the disciples have complete authority over these things. But, I would contend, what they do not have authority over is the human response to their mission. This is perhaps why Jesus is not as optimistic as the disciples when he charges them to rejoice, not in the subjugation of opposing spirits, but that they themselves have their "names recorded in heaven" (Luke 10:20). In other words, there will be much rejection (Luke 10:16) but they should rejoice that they are not part of that crowd. They are those who are partakers of the message and have their names written in heaven for it.

So once again, did Satan fall? According to the bible the answer is "yes," although the timing and nature of such a fall is still in question. It could be either past tense, future tense, or it simply means that when the gospel of the kingdom is preached Satan and all his associated powers and beings are falling over and over again. Or maybe it is a combination of these. Outside the world of the bible, the Church, and organized religion, Jeffery Burton Russell reminds us that "Few educated people today take the concept of the Devil seriously."[66] Stephen F. Noll however would prompt us to remember that "Education and wisdom are not the same thing" as he calls us to look deeper at the underlying causes of evil and to take Satan seriously.[67] It seems logical enough that inexplicable evil in the world has a powerful being opposed to God behind it, and that, consistent with a religious worldview, "Satan exists as a real supernatural person."[68] Christian theology in particular so much centers around the high point of God becoming the incarnate one in Christ, that it is not unreasonable to think that evil is embodied in the sort of incarnation that we have seen of Satan, who started off as an adversary in the heavenly court of God but eventually and rebelliously came into his own as the one opposed to God who leads his own malevolent kingdom.

The idea of Satan became so popular in the intertestamental and New Testament periods that we see him appearing in the form of other personalities in both pseudepigraphical literature and the New Testament. Origins for these alternate titles can sometimes be found in the Old Testament. For instance, king Ahaziah of Israel inquires of the Philistine god of Ekron for a solution to his illness rather than seeking after Yahweh and is strongly rebuked by the prophet Elijah for doing so (2 Kgs 1:1-6). The name of this god, "Baal-zebub," who is also named similarly "Beelzebub(l)," in the New Testament (Matt 10:25; 12:24,27, Mark 3:22, Luke 11:15, 18-19) becomes a name for Satan as can be seen in Jesus' debate with the Pharisees regarding his ability to cast out demons (Matt 12:22-29). It is certainly pejorative, as the Jews rejected the Philistine gods and made this particular one, literally, "the lord of the flies" as an insult because of the pesty insects' fondness for feasting on excrement. Thus was the Jewish view of the god of Ekron. In the pseudepigraphical *Testament of Solomon*, written of course prior to the New Testament, "Beelzebul" appears as a fallen prince of demons who was formerly a leading heavenly angel associated with the planet Venus thus reminding us of our Lucifer myth and the perceived satanic fall from heaven (Test Sol 6:1-3).[69] This gives us further background to Jesus' conversation with the Pharisees regarding the now established kingdom of Satan, aka "Beelzebul" (Matt 12:26). Also originating from the Old Testament is the word "Belial" (aka "Beliar"), which Paul uses in his Corinthian correspondence one time (2 Cor 6:15) to compare Christ with the devil. The phrase "sons of Belial" appears fifteen times in the Old Testament and means "worthless," that is to say, "worthless people," as in the case of the sons of Eli (1 Sam 2:12). In the intertestament, this too became a name for Satan. And yet another name for Satan in the intertestamental period was "Azazel," a word actually found three times in the Old Testament, all in Leviticus 16:7-10. In its Levitical context, Azazel refers either to the goat that was sent into the wilderness on the Day of Atonement to carry the peoples' sins away, or it refers to the actual wilderness place itself, a wasteland where refuse and that which was profane could be placed. However, in the intertestamental *Apocalypse of Abraham* Azazel (aka

"Azazael") is an unclean bird which came down upon the sacrifice
of Abraham that is found in Gen 15:11 (Apoc Abr 13:4-9) and
appears to have an evil dominion over the world (Apoc Abr 20:5). [70]
In the book of *Enoch*, Azazel is a leader of the Watchers of pre-
flood times who was responsible for teaching the world warfare,
witchcraft, and idolatry and to him all sin is to be ascribed (1 Enoch
8:1-10:8). [71] Another name for Satan not found in the Old Testament but in the later Rabbinic writings is "Samael" (aka "Sam-
mael"), a name which means "poison of God." Samael is an archangel who has similar Satan like functions as an accuser. In the
Kabbalah he is the serpent who tempts Eve, seduces and impreg-
nates her with Cain, and then becomes the consort of Adam's first
wife, Lilith, the mysterious being that we explore in chapter three
of this book. [72]

FALLEN ANGELS, EVIL SPIRITS, AND DEMONS

Thus Satan has come a long way since first seeing him rather subtly
in the Old Testament books of Zechariah and Job. Whether or not
he should be associated with Lucifer of Isa 14:12 fame is complete-
ly in doubt. In fact, the term "fallen angel" does not appear in the
bible at all although there are certain texts that could point in this
direction. The Rev 12 passage of which we have already spoken is
questionable because the apocalyptic flavor of the text is not a
straightforward narrative of some past event regarding a heavenly
rebellion. The tail of the dragon sweeping away one third of the
stars may be a reference to this sort of occurrence, or again, it may
not be (Rev 12:4). Also, the throwing down of the dragon may be
reflective of a pristine fall of Satan, or it may be peculiar to the
heavenly combat that is the background and context of the book of
Revelation (Rev 12:9), most obviously, and most likely, Roman
oppression. But there are some other New Testament texts which
speak of God being so infuriated at a certain band of angels that he

immediately cast them away into prison (1 Pet 3:19-20, 2 Pet 2:4, Jude v.6). What these verses share in common is a context of the other worldly incarceration taking place in association with days of antiquity and the sins of Sodom and Gomorrah. This then brings us back to Gen 6:1-4 regarding the "sons of God" having intercourse with the "daughters of men," a strange story that is greatly elaborated upon in the intertestamental period, particularly regarding the "Watchers," the fallen angels who entangled themselves illicitly with human females and committed sexual deviancy. These stories get serious attention in *1 Enoch 6-9* and the Qumran *Book of Giants*. It is possible that this is where the dis-embodied spirits in the bible originate. We read in the New Testament of evil/unclean spirits and demons, the apparent minions of Satan's kingdom, the kingdom Jesus spoke of in Matt 12:26. Yet we are never told where these spirits and demons come from. They are shadowy, murky, and mysterious beings. Are they the result of this mysterious union between sexually active angels and human females? Or, are they themselves fallen angels? However, the Peter and Jude texts have a cast of angels in bondage that are not free to roam because of their sexual crimes. It seems less likely that demons and the like are themselves angels who have fallen from their place in heaven because of this. It may be argued then that demons and spirits that may be called evil, unclean, or dis-embodied, particularly in the New Testament, are a result of the unholy union between the band of mischievous angels and women that is spoken of in Gen 6:1-4 and referred to over and over again in the Psedeupigrapha. Outside of Deut 32:17, Ps 106:7 and Isa 13:21; 34:14, there is very little demonic activity to be seen in the Old Testament. The Deuteronomy and Psalms passages are simply referring to false gods receiving sacrifice as demonic and the two Isaiah texts are most commonly translated as some sort of "shaggy goat" or "hairy being." However, in the New Testament demons and unclean spirits are mentioned sixty three times. This is a remarkable difference. The intertestamental period witnessed the development and abundance of increased demonic activity, much of which can be traced to the "sons of God" siring the "Nephilim" in Gen 6:1-4. Yet, if the world of demons is a result of that strange race of giants known as the Nephilim who became spirits without bodies after the Noah flood, then why are they so unheard from during the remainder of the rather lengthy Old Testament period? Although curiously, Jesus spoke of unclean spirits seeking a bodily home while wanting to pass through "waterless places" (Matt 12:43). Could this be a left-over fear of floods and water by these now dis-embodied giants who were judged by the deluge in Noah's day? In sum, there is not a straightforward answer on this matter, as the world of fallen angels and demon spirits remains a special mystery in the drama of scripture.

OTHER MYSTERIOUS SPIRITUAL ENTITIES

Besides bad angels, demons, evil/dis-embodied/unclean spirits making a strong appearance in the New Testament, there is an entirely different kind of category of mysterious entities written about in the New Testament, particularly by Paul, that are even more difficult to define. We see on a number of occasions terminology such as: "principalities, powers, rulers, authorities, dominions, and thrones." Paul seems to apply these categories to both earthly, natural, human powers as well as to heavenly and supernatural powers (Rom 8:37-39, Col 1:16; 2:15, Titus 3:1), especially in the letter to the Ephesians where the Church's battle occurs in "heavenly places" (Eph 1:20-21; 3:10-11; 6:10-12). Paul never defines these things, and it may be assumed that his first century audience would be clued in to what he was talking about. He argues in his writings that Christ and his Church have authority over these things and Paul's numerous terms may be another way of saying what Jesus spoke of in Luke 10:19 when he used authoritative language over "serpents, scorpions, and all the power of the enemy." The kingdom of Satan is indeed mysterious, but according to the bible, it is out there, it is real, and it seeks harm to Christ's kingdom.

Antithetically, Christ's kingdom has its own mysterious entities that are non-human and are involved in protecting and advancing Christ's cause. Angels make numerous appearances in the bible and is a study all of its own, well beyond what is intended in this work. One would note that there is especially frequent angelic activity during the ministry of Jesus. Angels announce Jesus' birth (Luke 1:11-20; 2:8-14), they serve to protect Jesus' in the temptation stories (Matt 4:6, Luke 4:10), and they are involved in the resurrection (Matt 28:2-6). Also, angels are portrayed as accompanying Jesus' at his return in glory (Matt 25:31). Two of the more significant ones are actually given names—Gabriel and Michael. At times in the Old Testament, Yahweh himself is not to be distinguished from what is called "the angel of Yahweh (the Lord)" (e.g. Gen 16:7-14). This sort of softening of terminology could have been for the purpose of lessening the danger in theophany encounters because it was common understanding that to be confronted by Yahweh would result in the death of the human. It was a way to mediate the divine encounter in language that could allow the person to survive after having come into the presence of the divine.[73] Mysterious, angelic type beings who are in support of God and his mission can be found at the outset of the biblical drama, such as the cherubim in the garden of Eden (Gen 3:24) and above the mercy seat (Heb 9:5), the seraphim ("burning ones") attending to God in the heavenly temple (Isa 6:1-8), and in Ezekiel's other-worldly visions (Ezek 1), as well as in the writings of John of the Apocalypse (Rev 4:4-8).

SUMMARY

Our study of Lucifer has demonstrated that this very term, although occurring in the bible only in the Latin translation of Isa 14:12, has been embellished and has taken on a life of its own well beyond its intended meaning of the taunt against the king of Babylon in Isaiah's oracle. The same could be said for Ezekiel's oracle against the king of Tyre in Ezek 28:12-19, which in popular interpretation today is often seen as a literal fall of Satan that corresponds with the Lucifer of Isa 14:12. The less murky figure of a supernatural being that is in opposition to God in the Old Testament is of course Satan, the very name of which means "adversary." Yet there is still much obscurity and mystery around the person of Satan in the Old Testament as he only makes a few appearances: Zech 3:1, Job 1-2, and perhaps 1 Chron 21:1. He would seem to be a part of God's royal court who serves the purpose of being an adversary and tester of God's people. Other nations outside of Israel wrestled with the problem of evil and almost certainly contributed to Israel's understanding and formation of the person of Satan. However, it is not until the intertestament that one begins to notice a Satan who is taking on a life of his own in complete rebellion against God and leading his own host of cohorts in spiritual battle. Jewish pseudepigraphical books such as: *Jubilees, 1 Enoch, Testament of Solomon, the Book of Giants, the Damascus Covenant* and *The Apocalypse of Abraham* all bear witness to this by speaking about Satan-like characters such as: Mastema, Beelzebub, Belial, Azazel, and Samael. By the time of the New Testament synoptic gospels, Satan is also known as the devil. He is still the accuser he was in the Old Testament and he takes on Jesus in the wilderness temptation, a battle he loses, indicative of his eventual fate. The Gospel of John portrays a Satan who is behind the scenes, working through human opponents of Jesus, but nonetheless tempting Jesus in a similar manner to the wilderness temptation. Paul expands our knowledge of Satan by showing him to be not only the adversary and tester of Old Testament fame, but also one who hinders, schemes, tests, and punishes. Satan's role is expanding in the New Testament, and by the Apocalypse he is in full spiritual combat with God and is associated with the devil, the serpent of old, and a great dragon. He represents the enemies of Christ's people, whether they be earthly opponents such as organized religion and political forces, or creatures in the cosmos warring against God's kingdom. A genuine biblical biography of Satan may be different from the biography that has developed in church tradition, thanks in no small part to the writings of the Church Father Origen who may have mis-represented Satan's story by connecting him to Lucifer and his fall. But whatever the case, even if the idea of Lucifer has become something well beyond what was intended in the biblical narrative, there is little doubt that the biblical message is to be well aware of the activities of one known as Satan and the devil who has a kingdom of spirits, beings, and entities who are not for the welfare of God's creation. Even so, that is not the total story regarding the strange and the mysterious of the spiritual world of creatures in the bible. On the side of good and God are archangels, angels, living beings, cherubim, and seraphim, all of which are involved in the cosmic conflict that will eventually result in the defeat of evil and chaos and the establishment of God's righteous and everlasting kingdom.

NOTES

1. Michael W. Ford, *Beginning Luciferian Magick* (Houston, TX: Succubus Productions, 2008).

2. The Latin word "Lucifer" is found in four other places in the Vulgate: Job 11:17; 38:32, Ps 110:3, and 2 Pet 1:19. None of these are a reference to a person or being.

3. Even Jesus calls himself "star of the morning" (Rev 22:16).

4. John D.W. Watts, *Isaiah 1-33 (Word Biblical Commentary)* (Waco, Tx.: Word Books, 1985), p.203.

5. John Goldingay, *The Theology of the Book of Isaiah* (Downers Grove, Ill.: IVP Academic, 2014), p.41.

6. John Oswalt, *The Book of Isaiah Chapters 1-39 (The New International Commentary on the Old Testament)* (Grand Rapids, Mi.: William B. Eerdmans Publishing Company, 1986), p.314.

7. Although Ronald Clements suggests that the original intention may have been for an Assyrian, not Babylonian, king. Ronald E. Clements, *Isaiah 1-39 (The New Century Bible Commentary)* (Grand Rapids, Mi.: William B. Eerdmans Publishing Company, 1980), p.139.

8. Oswalt, *The Book of Isaiah*, p.321.

9. Watts, *Isaiah 1-33*, p.209.

10. Goldingay, *The Theology of the Book of Isaiah*, p.42.

11. Clements, *Isaiah 1-39*, p.142.

12. Ibid.

13. George B. Gray, *Isaiah I-XXVII (The International Critical Commentary)* (Edinburgh: T&T Clark, 1975), p.255.

14. Clements, *Isaiah 1-39*, p.142.

15. Watts, *Isaiah 1-33*, p.212.

16. Ibid.

17. Ibid.

18. Oswalt, *The Book of Isaiah*, p.320.

19. "Lucifero" is found in *Hell*, Book 31, line 143 and Book 34, line 89. Ernest Hatch Wilkins and Thomas Goddard Bergin, *A Concordance to the Divine Comedy of Dante Alighieri* (Cambridge Ma.: The Belknap Press of Harvard University Press, 1965), p.300.

20. 1968, from the album *Beggars Banquet*.

21. This "council of the Lord" is understood in the Old Testament to be a literary device for metaphorical purposes regarding the ability to know the divine mind. For more, confer with such texts as: Gen 1:26, 1 Kgs 22:19-23, Job 1-2, Isa 6:8-11, Jer 23:18.

22. Adele Berlin and Marc Zvi Brettler, *The Jewish Study Bible Tanakh Translation* (Oxford, New York: Oxford University Press, 2004), p.1506.

23. A parallel text can be found in Ps 109:1-6 where the Psalmist has accusers desiring to slander him. However, there is no definite article before the word "satan" as there is in Zech 3:1.

24. G.H.Twelftree, *New Dictionary of Biblical Theology* (Leicester, England and Downers Grove, Ill.: InterVarsity Press, 2000), p.797.

25. Ibid.

26. Ibid. There is no evidence in Ancient Israel or in the larger Mesopotamian area that there was ever a legal office of an accuser, or what might be known in the West as a "prosecuting attorney."

27. Berlin and Brettler, *The Jewish Study Bible*, p.1506.

28. T.J. Wray and Gregory Mobley, *The Birth of Satan: Tracing the Devil's Biblical Roots* (New York, NY.: Palgrave Macmillan, 2005), p.51.

29. Wray and Mobley use the language "terrestrial adversary" to refer to "satan" as a human or military opponent and "angelic adversary" for "satan" as an other-worldly being. Wray and Mobley, *The Birth of Satan*, pp. 52,57.

30. Berlin and Brettler, *The Jewish Study Bible*, p.1751.

31. Ronald F. Youngblood, *1, 2 Samuel (The Expositor's Bible Commentary)* (Frank E. Gaebelein, Gen. Ed., vol.3) (Grand Rapids, Mi.: Zondervan, 1992), p.1096. See also J. Barton Payne, *1, 2 Chronicles (The Expositor's Bible Commentary)* (Frank E. Gaebelein, Gen. Ed., vol.4) (Grand Rapids, Mi.: Zondervan, 1988), p.407.

32. Wray and Mobley, *The Birth of Satan*, p.64.

33. Ibid., pp.67-68.

34. O.S. Wintermute, *Jubilees (The Old Testament Pseudepigrapha)* (James H. Charlesworth, Gen. Ed., vol.2) (New York, NY.: Doubleday, 1985), p.90.

35. Ibid., p.91.

36. Wray and Mobley, *The Birth of Satan*, p.102.

37. Ibid., p.99.

38. Ibid., p.106.

39. Ibid., p.75.

40. Ibid., p.101.

41. Ibid., pp.95-96.

42. Ibid., p.96.

43. Herbert Lockyer, *Satan: His Person & Power* (Waco, Tx.: Word Books, 1980), p.17.

44. Henry Ansgar Kelly, *Satan: A Biography* (Cambridge: Cambridge University Press, 2006), p.168.

45. Wray and Mobley, *The Birth of Satan*, p.115.

46. Elaine Pagels, *The Origin of Satan* (New York, NY.: Random House Inc., 1995), p.179.

47. Wray and Mobley, *The Birth of Satan*, p.115.

48. Ibid., p.123.

49. Ibid., p.128.

50. Ibid., p.126.

51. Frederick William Danker, *A Greek-English Lexicon of the New Testament and other Early Christian Literature* (3rd edition, BDAG) (Chicago and London: The University of Chicago Press, 2000), p.555.

52. Fritz Rienecker and Cleon Rogers, *Linguistic Key to the Greek New Testament* (Grand Rapids, Mi.: Zondervan Publishing House, 1976) p. 593.

53. Kelly, *Satan: A Biography*, p.171.

54. *1 Enoch* 6-10.

55. *Jubilees* 5.

56. Wray and Mobley, *The Birth of Satan*, p.136.

57. Ibid., p.137.

58. Ibid., p.140.

59. This episode concerning the dispute between Michael and the devil was perhaps contained in the lost ending of the *Testament of Moses* or perhaps the cognate work known as *The Assumption of Moses*, although there is no certain conclusion. J. Priest, *Testament of Moses (The Old Testament Pseudepigrapha)*

(James H. Charlesworth, Gen. Ed., vol.1) (New York, NY.: Doubleday, 1983), p.924.

60. Kelly, *Satan: A Biography*, pp.191-214.

61. Ibid., p.8.

62. Ibid., p.199.

63. Ibid., p.191.

64. Ibid., p.198.

65. Ibid., p.203.

66. Jeffery Burton Russell, *The Prince of Darkness: Radical Evil and the Power of Good in History* (Itbaca and London: Cornell University Press, 1988), p.2.

67. Stephen F. Noll, *Angels of Light, Powers of Darkness: Thinking Biblically About Angels, Satan & Principalities* (Downers Grove, Ill.: InterVarsity Press, 1998) p.96.

68. Kelly, *Satan: A Biography*, p.168.

69. D.C. Duling, *Testament of Solomon (The Old Testament Pseudepigrapha)* (James H. Charlesworth, Gen. Ed., vol.1) (New York, NY.: Doubleday, 1983), p.967.

70. H.G. Lunt, *The Apocalypse of Abraham (The Old Testament Pseudepigrapha)* (James H. Charlesworth, Gen. Ed., vol.1) (New York, NY.: Doubleday, 1983), p.695, 699.

71. E. Isaac, *1 Enoch (The Old Testament Pseudepigrapha)* (James H. Charlesworth, Gen. Ed., vol.1) (New York, NY.: Doubleday, 1983), pp.16-18.

72. For further information please visit: http://www.jewishencylopedia.com/articles/13055-samael

73. Twelftree, *New Dictionary of Biblical Theology*, p.796.

Chapter Two

Leviathan

We now return to the book of Isaiah where we were introduced to Lucifer and begin to investigate our second primary mysterious creature of the bible—Leviathan. Leviathan is found in just a few places in the bible and only one time in Isaiah. The verse in question, Isa 27:1, begins the concluding chapter of what is commonly referred to as "the Isaianic apocalypse,"[1] a section that includes chs.24-27 following the larger section of oracles against nations in chs.13-23 where the Lucifer text is found. It might be argued however that 27:1 actually belongs as the concluding verse to ch.26, just prior to the new section on the song of the vineyard. Whatever the case may be, this Leviathan text serves as a summation of the defeat of all enemies of Israel that have been envisioned throughout the oracles against the nations and the Isaianic apocalypse and is as much eschatological as it is apocalyptic. The verse reads, "On that day the Lord with his cruel and great and strong sword will punish Leviathan the fleeing Serpent, Leviathan the twisting serpent, and he will kill the dragon that is in the sea."[2]

SERPENTS & SEA MONSTERS

There is a certain amount of synthetic parallelism going on in Isa
27:1 with its double mention of the Leviathan creature being as a
variously described serpent as well as a dragon or monster of the
sea. To help us understand Leviathan the sea creature, it would be
helpful to say a few words about serpents and sea monsters, creatures that also have their place in the bible and serve as parallel to,
or synonymous with, Leviathan.

Serpents, although not unanimously highlighted in the bible as
negative creatures, such as is the case with the staff of Moses
turning into a serpent (Exod 4:3; 7:10-12) and the healing that
Moses' bronze serpent brought (Num 21:9), connote evil, terror,
and fear in the biblical world. The physical features of serpents like
slithering movements, stealth, lightning speed, venomous bites,
camouflage, and general deception are an ever present reminder of
danger, and in a theological sense, represent not only the trickery of
an enemy, but the potential judgment of God. Snakes hide in walls
(Eccles 10:8, Amos 5:19), bite without warning (Gen 49:17), and
hatch eggs which will only lead to greater evil and danger (Isa
59:5). Such fear and respect led to deifying them in numerous
contexts. "The worship of the serpent/snake is found in all ancient
religions, even in India and further east."[3] This is certainly the case
in Canaan itself, where serpents were worshipped out of fear that
the serpent would bring destructive chaos and evil. "Figurines of
Asherah, the fertility goddess, were often draped with representations of snakes, as were her altars."[4] The creation epics of Mesopotamia involve serpents in sinister ways, as for instance in the Gilgamesh Epic where a serpent robs Gilgamesh of a fragment of a
sacred plant which keeps him from gaining eternal life. And although there is no serpent like creature discussed in the first two
chapters of Genesis that are threatening God's newly created cosmic order, there is a more subtle entrance onto the stage of a talking
serpent in Gen 3. It is here that the biblical narrative changes from a

place of human harmony with God in the Garden of Eden to a place of sin, fall, and death. Although Christian theology makes an immediate connection with the serpent being the devil in disguise, Old Testament Israelite theology did not necessarily make such a connection. The Israelites did not attempt to see all evil embodied in one being who was the ultimate source or cause of all evil. "In fact, it would appear that the author of Genesis is intentionally underplaying the role or identification of the serpent."[5] Just as we saw the development of Satan taking shape during the intertestamental period, so also the association of the serpent with Satan takes place during this time period. "The earliest extant reference to any association is found in *Wisdom of Solomon* 2:23-24 (first century B.C.): ' . . . but through the devil's envy death entered the world . . . "[6] In the New Testament we see the continuing power of Jesus on earth as his disciples would be able to handle deadly serpents without the use of charms or fear of being hurt (Mark 16:18). This is evidenced in the life of Paul who shakes off a snake bite without a problem and then is promptly elevated to god-like status (Acts 28:1-6). As seen earlier in Luke 10:19 the disciples of Christ would have "authority to tread upon serpents and scorpions and over all the power of the enemy." Although Old Testament Israel did not connect the serpent to Satan the New Testament Christian Church did. This can be seen in other texts such as Rom 16:20 where Paul, in apparent resonance with the cursing of the serpent in Gen 3:15 states to the Roman Christians that "the God of peace will soon crush Satan under your feet." But it is most evident in a verse which we have referenced before, Rev 12:9, where "the serpent of old" is also called "the devil and Satan." As regards our main concern in this study, biblical theology teaches us that whereas serpents are evil representations of the devil himself, all evil shall be overcome in God's kingdom illustrated by such prophetic words as "And the nursing child will play by the hole of the cobra, and the weaned child will put his hand on the viper's den" (Isa 11:8).

The Old Testament in particular speaks, not only of serpents but also of sea monsters, sometimes translated as "dragons" or even "serpents." This is to be found in the opening chapter of the bible where on the fifth day of creation God created "sea monsters," translated from the Hebrew תנין (Gen 1:21). Unlike the creation epics of cultures which surrounded ancient Israel, this creation account reveals no struggle between God and the sea monsters he created. He is in complete control of the forces of chaos, fear, and danger. In fact, as far as Israel is concerned these sea monsters are to praise Yahweh (Ps 148:7). The prophets of Israel associated sea monsters with empires and their leaders. For Jeremiah this was Nebuchadnezzar of Babylon (Jer 51:34) and for Ezekiel this was the Pharaoh of Egypt (Ezek 29:3; 32:2). In fact, Job saw himself as being treated by Yahweh as a sea monster that Yahweh was keeping an eye on as well as imprisoned (Job 7:12). His sarcasm and cynicism tell of how the sea monsters were wild creatures, not to be trusted. So the sea monster motif in the bible can be applied to people, empires, and actual water creatures. In Ps 74:13-14 the sea monsters and the Leviathan are close in association. We shall visit this verse in a moment. But for now, we return to Isa 27:1 for a brief examination of the language of the text surrounding the Leviathan creature.

Isaiah 27:1 reaches backward to the past and forward to the future. The beginning of the verse, "In that day," is eschatological in nature and envisions a conflict in which Yahweh destroys Israel's enemies and all evil in a day to come. The remainder of the verse, with its Leviathan and sea monster imagery, resonates with the primordial conflict worldview of many of the ancient near eastern cultures regarding the creation of the world. More specifically, in the Ugaritic literature the god Baal destroyed a mythological dragon of chaos named Lotan who represented the powers of the sea and of the deep.[7] The Ugaritic language is built on a tri-lateral root system, as is Hebrew, and both languages share the same three consonants for the root word of their sea monster. The similarity is far too great to be coincidence and one can only conclude that the Israelite and Ugaritic cultures cross pollinated on matters of religion and myth. In the same way in Babylonia the killing of the sea monster Tiamat precedes Marduk's accession to sovereign powers.[8] Christopher Seitz sees Leviathan in Isa 27:1 as "a cipher of Babylon,"[9] and John D.W. Watts equates Leviathan with the city of Tyre because of its trade activity on the sea.[10] G.B. Gray notes that rabbis and scholars have suggested identifying the Leviathans of Isa 27:1 with various empires because of the bodies of water associated with those empires. For instance, because the first Leviathan is described as "fleeing," this could be a possible reference to Assyria that is situated on the Tigris, a river that is rushing and rapid. The second Leviathan, described in the text as "twisting" could be Babylon, located on the Euphrates, a river which is characterized by many turns and labyrinth-like windings. Egypt on the Nile and bordering the Mediterranean Sea would be indicated by the sea monster mentioned at the end of Isa 27:1.[11] The suggestions are varied and many, and could include the Persian Empire as well. Oswalt understands the threefold mentioning of Leviathan (one of which is "sea monster") as "simply a poetic convention in the Canaanite area."[12] There is therefore according to him no need to make clear identifications with specific nations. In support of this interpretation Robert Fyall states, "Leviathan here sums up all that is evil and opposed to God, no matter if its earthly manifestation is Assyria, Babylon, Edom or any other power."[13]

Another possible way to understand the three fold description of the Leviathan sea monster in Isa 27:1 is to recognize that it is a poetic way of emphasizing the above point, that there is evil and opposition to God everywhere and that the fleeing serpent is raised in the air and ready to strike, the twisted serpent is coiled on the ground and ready to strike, and the monster of the sea is just that, a sea going creature of terror. In sum, Leviathan and what it represents is to be found in air, on land, and on sea. There is no escaping the influence of evil in the world. The whole of creation is infested with alien, evil powers which will be sought out and destroyed no matter where they are.[14] This is the death of Leviathan, "the monster of moral evil."[15] This is ultimately the vision of the bible. John Goldingay states, "Leviathan is an Old Testament way of referring to the being called Satan in later Jewish writings and in the New Testament."[16] For Isaiah, a prophet of ancient Israel, this was a way to portray resistance to God at a time when there was no consistent terminology or systematic portrayal of evil that might be seen today with Satan as the embodiment of evil.

We can now return to Ps 74:13-14 and its mentioning of Leviathan. The Psalmist here is lamenting the devastation of the homeland by a foreign enemy who has even destroyed the sanctuary of Yahweh and the meeting places (vv.3-4; 7-8). But then there is remembrance of the God of old who brought creation out of chaos (vv.12-17). In the midst of this memory Yahweh "didst crush the heads of Leviathan (v.14)," which has been brought into parallelism with Yahweh's "breaking the heads of the sea monsters" (v.13). If God can do this then he certainly is capable of restoring the nation from its plunder. It is as if Israel has returned to primordial chaos and the God who subdued such in creation would be capable of doing it again to restore the nation. The enemy who has done this to Israel is the earthly counterpart to Leviathan, but they will be broken and crushed even as Leviathan was.[17]

Leviathan is also mentioned in Ps 104:26. The Psalmist blesses Yahweh for his creative acts in this psalm and expresses this with a poetic description of creation that serves as a nice supplement to the more prose creation accounts of Gen 1-2. The sea is mentioned here more as a thing of beauty, peace, and tranquility, even as it is in Gen 1, rather than a place of conflict and chaos that might be found in other ancient near eastern origin stories. As in Gen 1:21 where the sea monsters are under God's control, so also here the

Leviathan and all the sea are under his control. Indeed, we see a description of Leviathan here that is unlike any of the other mentioning of Leviathan in the Old Testament. The sea creature is tame, calm, peaceful, and playful, more like a pet to God rather than a dangerous creature to be feared. The lightness of Leviathan here reinforces the greatness of God and his control over all things.

The picture of Leviathan in the book of Job however is quite a different matter. The ferocious creature is untamable and cannot be leashed (Job 40:29, Eng. 41:5). Leviathan is first mentioned in Job during Job's lament over the events of chs. 1-2 where he curses the day of his birth and likens his story to "the rousing of Leviathan" (Job 3:8). In modern parlance, the phrase might be compared to "let sleeping dogs lie." Had Job never been born such trouble would not have arisen. The day of his birth should be obliterated. After this, Leviathan is not mentioned again in the book of Job until ch.41 where the creature is given some detailed attention.[18] In a literal sense, commentators have attempted to identify Leviathan as the whale, crocodile, or even a dinosaur. Such naturalistic interpretations may or may not have some credibility, but surely fall short of the supernatural and poetic intention of the Leviathan creature, which is most likely a "guise for Satan."[19] The Satan who is so much a part of the opening scenes of the Job drama in chs. 1-2 has dropped out of the story line; but in reality, he has reared his head as the Leviathan seen in 3:8 and ch.41. Leviathan is a formidable foe, as is Satan. The rhetorical question of Job 40:25 (Eng. 41:1), "Can you draw out Leviathan with a fishhook?" has an obvious answer—"no!," the sum of which is that the problem of evil, chaos, fear, and suffering in the world has no easy answer. The clear implication of the chapter is that only God can handle this. He is the tamer of Leviathan, the defeater of Satan, and the one who may celebrate the "moral triumph over the forces of evil."[20]

BEHEMOTH & RAHAB

Just prior to the description of Leviathan near the end of the book
of Job there is a description of a similar creature, Behemoth, a
creature of the land (Job 40:15-24). The Hebrew feminine plural
ending of this noun is likely a plural of majesty, that is, this creature
represents the greatest of land animals. Behemoth is the beast par
excellence. There is no land creature like her. Similar to Leviathan,
Behemoth is given an elaborate physical description of power and
strength. A common naturalistic interpretation is that Behemoth is
the hippopotamus, a great animal of both land and river. But once
again, to leave the meaning of this beast at a natural and scientific
level only is to fall one very important step short of grasping the
intended purpose of the writer of the poetic book of Job. Behemoth
should also be seen as an image of those things in the supernatural
world which strike terror in the hearts of humans. Like Leviathan,
the great water animal, so Behemoth, the great land animal, reinforces the notion that humans are not immune from disease, death,
chaos, disorder, and evil of every imaginable kind. Such enemies
are found on land and are found at sea. It is not that Behemoth and
Leviathan are merely the hippopotamus and crocodile respectively,
or some other animals such as the whale or a dinosaur, but they
belong to two worlds, the world of the natural and the world of the
supernatural.[21] Behemoth has some similarities to the Canaanite
god Mot, the god of death, and thereby might represent this ultimate enemy of humans in the Israelite mind.[22] However, of the two
creatures Leviathan carries the greatest weight, not only for being
originally aroused in Job 3:8, or because the Israelites tended to
fear the sea, but also because Leviathan serves as the climax to all
Job is struggling against in this story in the penultimate chapter of
the book just prior to Job's restoration to conclude the book. The
satan, who seems to have disappeared since ch. 2 after causing all
the initial upheaval makes a showing at the end of the book of Job
as both the land creature Behemoth and the sea creature Leviathan.

And as the Leviathan cannot be brought up from the depths of the sea with a simple and flimsy fishhook, so also the Behemoth cannot be easily snared and led off captive with a hook through the nose (Job 40:24). In a word, there are no easy answers to the difficulty and mystery of suffering, chaos, and evil in the world, as Job has found out. As can be seen in the numerous rhetorical questions of Yahweh from ch. 38 until the end of the book, the answers to these questions belong to him and him alone.

Another mysterious creature mentioned in the Hebrew Bible is Rahab. Rahab is to be found in only the same three books in which Leviathan is found: Isaiah, Psalms, and Job. In the two Isaiah references, Isa 30:7 and Isa 51:9, Rahab is a code term for Egypt. So also in the two Psalms references, Ps 87:4 and Ps 89:10, Rahab is again a code term for Egypt. This is very straightforward. The Egyptian empire is depicted as a beast for smaller nations like Israel to contend with. Like Leviathan, Rahab was a creature of the deep, the sea monster of popular legend which played a role in popular thought.[23] In the Isaiah texts Rahab is defeated by Yahweh. The same is true of the Ps 89:10 reference. Egypt may look as fearsome as a great sea creature but instead is powerless against God. In Job 26:12 the shattering of Rahab takes place in a creation poem where Yahweh defeats chaos, which may or may not be a reflection back on God's defeat of Pharaoh's Egypt. Rahab as a code term for Egypt is not the case in the first reference found in the book of Job. This text reads "God does not restrain his anger; even the cohorts of Rahab cowered at his feet" (Job 9:13, NIV). It is another poetic account of Yahweh's victory over chaos in creation that plays off of common ancient near eastern origin stories.

DRAGONS, BEASTS, & CREATURES
OF APOCALYPTIC LITERATURE

As time moved along in the ancient near east so did the type of stories they told. By late in the Old Testament period a new type of genre was developing known as apocalyptic. A large body of literature followed that introduced new and strange ideas into popular thought of the day. One might recall that in recent western civilization the introduction of science fiction came about as a result of the rise of science and the industrial revolution. H.G. Wells book *War of the Worlds* in 1898 resonates with the idea of introducing a brand new genre as a result of changing times. The radio broadcast of *War of the Worlds* on October 30, 1938 narrated by Orson Welles allegedly caused a mass panic as people heard of a Martian invasion on planet earth that some believed was real. This was a result of unfamiliarity with the genre that was now being presented.

For its part, apocalyptic literature developed amongst Jews between 200 BCE and 100 CE and it is estimated that some seventy "apocalypses" were recorded.[24] During these days Jews of Palestine were occupied by the armies of those loyal to Hellenistic culture and the Romans. They penned apocalyptic as an oppressed subgroup seeking a better future reality beyond the present state of affairs.[25] They had become pessimistic about the present world and man's ability to overcome evil through better living.[26] "More comprehensive coverage was needed"[27] to "grasp the laws which governed the world"[28] and to re-establish that God was still in control of things. Whereas the prophets of Israel spoke the word of God as mouthpieces of the divine voice with "thus sayeth the Lord" and similar utterances, apocalyptic was a revelation by a "celestial personage"[29] who revealed secrets via dreams, visions, and various symbols, such as the use of numbers and mysterious creatures. They were not only concerned with the element of time and the future, but were also delving into the spatial arena where the cosmic fight between God and the forces of evil were taking place.

The basic definition of an apocalypse is a revealing of both time and space where heavenly secrets are disclosed about the end of the world, the defeat of evil, and the coming of the kingdom of God.[30] It showed that human kingdoms were short-lived and were becoming more and more beastly and less and less human as humans were designed to be.[31] This we shall see in the books of Daniel and Revelation. Apocalyptic proved especially helpful during times of persecution to bring comfort as it purported to have an ancient, authoritative voice, such as Daniel, predict the fall of empires.

EZEKIEL 1 & ISAIAH 6

Some of the first glimpses of apocalyptic that can be observed in the bible can be found in the opening chapter of the book of Ezekiel. The context of Ezekiel is the beginning stages of the Babylonian exile when Jews had to rethink everything they had known about their God and their sacred traditions. This time of turmoil led to the birth of apocalyptic, and although it will not be a full-blown phenomenon for a few centuries, apocalyptic was now in its infant stages. The person of Ezekiel is known for his unusual behavior and bizarre antics, which are not surprising when one considers the difficulty of the times and the grappling with the new, challenging hardships the Jews in exile had to face. It was a time of transition and turmoil and apocalyptic was in one sense, beginning to come to the rescue of the Jewish faith.

Ezekiel's prophecy starts out with a vision of an other-worldly storm with flashing lights and the likeness of glowing metal, torches, lightning flashes, crystal, and the colors of the rainbow. It was no doubt an awesome sight that could not be fully explained in human terms, hence Ezekiel's repetitive allusive language ("something like/likeness/appearance/resembling," vv.4, 5, 13, 16, 22, 24, 26, 27, 28). In fact, the modern Hebrew word for "electricity" is derived from the Hebrew word חַשְׁמַל in 1:4 that gets translated as "glowing metal" or "burnished bronze."[32] Brownlee calls the vision "technicolor, the only vision of a Hebrew prophet to be so described."[33] Ezekiel beholds mysterious creatures, "four living beings" (v.5) that are within the storm. These will later be described as "cherubim" (10:15, 20). What Ezekiel is beholding as a heavenly reality, both Moses and Solomon could only envision in artistic form, as God had instructed the great prophet and the great king to craft such images first on the ark of the covenant in Moses' day (Exod 25:18-22; 37:7-9) and then in the inner sanctuary of the temple in Solomon's day (1 Kgs 6:23-28, 2 Chron 3:10-14). These four living beings are described with great elaboration, but ultimately only to give way to the one with the appearance of a man who sits on the throne (vv.26-28). This of course is "the glory of the Lord" and it is what finally causes Ezekiel to fall on his face (1:28).

As for the four living beings though, they get the majority of attention in the chapter leading up to the one who sits on the throne. They had human form while at the same time having four different faces that travelled straight ahead without turning. One face was that of a man. To the right of this face was the face of a lion and to the left of this face was the face of a bull. On the reverse side of the human like face was the face of an eagle. These four faces speak of supremacy over different spheres of creation: humans are the highest of all God's creatures, the lion is king of wild animals, the bull is the greatest of domestic animals, and the eagle is supreme amongst the birds.[34] Also, these images would have certainly resonated with Ezekiel who sits by the rivers of Babylon well aware that four of the chief deities of Babylon were Nabu (the announcer, represented by the human face), Nergal, the god of the underworld and plague (represented by the lion), Marduk (represented by the bull), and Ninib, the god of the chase and war (represented by the eagle).[35] Ezekiel is being taught in the vision that the God of Israel is beyond all these so called Babylon gods.

To further describe the four living beings from the first chapter of Ezekiel, they had four wings with hands underneath the wings. Two of the wings touched the wings of another living being and two of the wings covered their bodies. They also had legs with calf hoofs. To accompany the living beings there were wheels in the middle of wheels with eyes all around the rims of the wheels. Whenever the living beings moved the wheels moved with them. Whenever the living beings flapped their wings the sound of it was majestic and roaring, described like the moving of many waters, or what we might imagine to be the sound of a mighty waterfall. Whenever the wings went still, the noised ceased as well. It had to be sensory overload for Ezekiel, of both sight and sound.

Israelite prophets such as Ezekiel were known for their great visions of God. What Ezekiel saw as recorded in chapter one has some similarities to what Isaiah saw as recorded in the sixth chapter of the book which bears his name. However, there are some important distinctions to be made as concerns the creatures that surrounded the throne of God. Whereas Ezekiel's living beings were cherubim, Isaiah's heavenly creatures were seraphim. Cherubim make other appearances in the Old Testament, for instance in the beginning of the biblical story when they served as guardians of the tree of life after the sin of Adam and Eve (Gen 3:24). However, seraphim show up in the Old Testament only in the heavenly throne room vision of Isa 6. They have hands and feet and six wings: two to cover their face, two to cover their feet, and two with which to fly. The covering of the face might suggest an unwillingness to look upon God because of his greatness and the covering of the feet might suggest a hiding oneself from God so as not to be seen by such holy eyes. Because the feet are at times in the Hebrew Bible a euphemism for the genitals, it might be a way to suggest that this part of the anatomy is often times used for less than holy purposes. Although it is questionable as to whether or not angelic type beings should be regarded as having reproductive organs. The covering of the feet might simply suggest humility in the presence of God. As far as looking at God is concerned, one might also keep in mind that the cherubim of Ezek 1 are never in a position to view God as their faces will only move straight ahead.[36] They apparently do not look upon the divine either. As for the wings which are not used to cover bodily parts, they can then be used for movement and for ministry. These are the functioning wings which allow these beings to be used of God.

R. E. Clements suggests that the seraphim might have had a serpent like form because the adjective "fiery" used to describe the serpents sent by God in Num 21:6 and mentioned again in Deut 8:15 is the word seraphim ("seraph" for the singular).[37] He states, "such creatures of mixed form were popular in Egyptian royal symbolism, where the winged cobra was a widely used symbol for a divine protective spirit guarding the king."[38] The seraphim are therefore like the cherubim who serve the function of protecting the throne of God.[39] For sure the seraphim can be described as fiery, or burning ones which burn bright, for that is the very definition of their name. Yet these creatures which shine so bright dare not look at the brightness of the glory of God.[40] It was for just such a violation that the prophet Isaiah announced his doom, "Woe is me . . . for my eyes have seen the king (Isa 6:5)." In sum, the seraphim of Isa 6 and the cherubim of Ezek 1 and elsewhere portray a variety of heavenly creatures which serve the purposes of God. This should be in no way surprising as one considers the magnitude, diversity, and variety of earthly creatures that surround us all in natural life.[41] This was part of the lesson that Job needed to learn as God took him on a rather mind bending tour of all that he has created and of all that Job was so much unaware (Job 38-41).

DANIEL & REVELATION

The greatest works of apocalyptic literature in the bible are of course Daniel in the Old Testament and Revelation in the New Testament. The book of Daniel is especially the prototype of what Jewish apocalyptic literature would come to be.[42] Here we find beasts and creatures of apocalyptic literature, but we do not find a place for the person of Satan,[43] as we shall find in the later book of Revelation. It may be that the character of Satan is hiding in Daniel behind other beasts and creatures, as he did under the suggested guise of Leviathan and Behemoth in the majority of the book of Job, because there are no direct references to him after Job 3.

Even though the beginning of the story line in the book of Daniel is against the backdrop of Nebuchadnezzar's Babylon, scholars debate whether the real context of the book should be placed in the second century BCE during the time of the Greek/Jewish war where Antiochus Epiphanes and his Hellenistic influences was the real source of concern for the original readers. This is some four hundred years removed from the Babylonian crises and would therefore make the book of Daniel more intertestament than it would Old Testament. Whatever the correct historical context of the book might be, it is very much on the cutting edge of the many Jewish apocalypses that were produced in the time shortly before Christ until the time shortly after Christ by Jewish communities.

As there are differences of opinions for Daniel's place in history, so there is also a difference of opinion regarding Daniel's place in the canon of both the Jewish and Christian sacred scriptures. For Jews, the Hebrew Bible places Daniel amongst the Historical Books, near the end of the canon. For Christians, the book of Daniel is categorized with the Prophets, following the writings of Isaiah, Jeremiah, and Ezekiel. There are theological reasons for this. Jews do not consider Daniel to fit the model of the classical Hebrew prophets who were custodians of the Mosaic covenant and preachers of repentance. But rather, Jews understand Daniel the

person to be a statesman, more in the manner of Joseph and Morde-
cai, both of whom served in important positions in foreign courts.
Daniel does not preach oracles and sermons to Israel as the classical prophets do, his visionary method is much bigger and international, and even universal in scale, and he considers kingdoms
more than he does the nation of Israel. Daniel fits well with the
prophets in the Christian canon however because prophets have
been viewed as messianic preachers by the Church, and Daniel has
visions of the "son of man," a messianic title of New Testament
notoriety. Whatever might be the proper placement of Daniel within the biblical canon, there is certainly theological uniqueness and
progressiveness with this rather short, yet powerful biblical book.

The book of Daniel has a very simple two part structure. Chapters 1-6 are narrative and chapters 7-12 are apocalyptic. The genre
is distinctively different once one reads the conclusion of chapter 6
and then moves on to chapter 7. It is somewhat like Dorothy in the
Wizard of Oz proclaiming to her dog Toto, "we're not in Kansas
anymore." Daniel 7-12 will feel like strange and unfamiliar territory to the reader, as Dorothy experienced. However, the message of
the two sections of Daniel is consistent in promoting a theology of
persecution at the hands of evil empires that shall ultimately collapse at the coming of God's kingdom. Whether the genre is story,
as in chapters 1-6, or apocalyptic, as in chapters 7-12, the message
and result are the same – stay faithful to God through persecution
and victory will be obtained in the end, because the real battle is
fought in the heavenly places and not on earth.

The opening chapter of the book of Daniel sets the stage for the
entire book by placing Daniel and his three colleagues in servitude
in the royal court of Babylon during the early period of the exile.
The theological message is clear. Daniel and his friends stay as
loyal as they can to their God and their distinctive Jewish ways
even in the midst of hostile and exiled circumstances. By the end of
the chapter, Nebuchadnezzar has already faded from view and Dan-

iel has survived into the reign of Cyrus, the next foreign potentate (Dan 1:21).

Chapter 2 returns to the early reign of Nebuchadnezzar and his famous dream of the multi-metaled statue. The head is made of gold, the upper body and arms made of silver, the mid-section and thighs are made of bronze, the legs of iron, and the feet a mixture of iron and clay. It is obvious that the metals are getting cheaper as one traverses down the statue from head to toe. Daniel rightly interprets the dream as Nebuchadnezzar's Babylon being the head of gold (Dan 2:38). After this, all else becomes speculation as far as what later kingdoms will be represented by what metals on the statue. The hindsight of history can give insight here because it is common knowledge that the empires to follow would include in chronological order: the Medes and the Persians, followed by the Greek and the Romans. Some of these kingdoms will be called out by name in the apocalyptic section. The theological message is that earthly kingdoms are on borrowed time and eventually won't have a leg to stand on, so to speak, as the impressive statue in the dream gets knocked down by a stone cut without human hands (Dan 2:34). The non-human touch to the destroying stone represents the divine element as opposed to the ever so human element of the building of the earthly kingdoms, and could even indicate the eventual incarnation of Jesus, including the virgin birth, and all that goes with Jesus and his kingdom coming supernaturally, in a way opposite of human kings. The supernatural demolishes the natural in the dream of the statue. The book of Daniel therefore anticipates the gospel of Jesus in its own unique way. The stone that struck the statue becomes a great mountain that fills the whole earth (Dan 2:35). The once formidable statue is crushed to chaff, only to be driven away by the wind without a trace (Dan 2:35). As the statue basically fell on its face, so Dan 2 concludes with Nebuchadnezzar falling on his face before Daniel and promoting Daniel within the kingdom of Babylon (Dan 2:46-49).

The famous fiery furnace incident of chapter 3 has a message consistent with chapter 2—earthly kingdoms are subject to a higher power. The statue has apparently motivated King Nebuchadnezzar to erect an image of gold that was rather gangly in dimension, which is ninety feet tall by nine feet wide, or, in other words, ten times as high as it was in width. Nebuchadnezzar did not get the point of the dream of the statue and its' interpretation in the preceding chapter. No doubt because he was the head of gold in the dream he now has this gold statue built to represent the greatness of his kingdom. It is of course a source of idolatry for Jews in that all the subjects of his kingdom were to pay homage to it. This will not be acceptable to Daniel's three loyalist Hebrew friends who find themselves thrown into a fiery furnace for non-compliance. They have resisted after the manner of Daniel in the opening chapter of the book. The appearance of a fourth man in the furnace "like a son of the gods" brings Nebuchadnezzar back to the humble position he was in at the conclusion of chapter two, as all three Jews survive unscathed into a prosperous future (Dan 3:30) and a fourth man, impressive in stature, is present with them in what should have been a sure death situation. [44]

Nebuchadnezzar has another dream in Dan 4 which is in need of interpretation. Daniel is once again able to do so, and the dream of a great tree the king saw which filled the whole earth to provide food, shelter, and shade is similar to the statue dream of chapter 2. The tree is specifically described as being "great in height" (Dan 4:10). Both images, the statue and the tree, are tall and impressive, just as the image of gold in chapter 3 was built to be a towering structure. Size and power of earthly kingdoms is a common theme here. But, just as the stone crashed into the base of the metal statue and brought it tumbling down, so also the tree is chopped down with nothing but a stump to remain (Dan 4:14-15). Nebuchadnezzar and his Babylonian kingdom is the felled tree and the stump which barely survives on into the future (Dan 4:19-27).

What is of peculiar interest for our concerns is the medium by which the tree is felled. It is a heavenly being of some sort who comes down from above to carry out the task of cutting down the tree. This being is known as a "watcher," which comes from the Aramaic עיר for one who has been awakened. It appears three times in chapter 4 (vv.13, 17, and 23). Each time, the watcher is associated with being a "holy one," a term which grants this being heavenly authority to pass sentence on Nebuchadnezzar and his kingdom. This is the only place in the Old Testament where this word "watcher" appears. We have however previously discussed this word as it appears in some of the pseudepigraphic books such as Jubilees and 1 Enoch, as well as in the Qumran literature. In these instances, the "watchers" have turned bad somehow, and are associated with rebelling against God, and one of them eventually becomes Satan himself. Back in the book of Daniel, these "watchers" are as mysterious as the one "like a son of the gods" in 3:25. It is not unimaginable that divinity is envisioned in both instances, but the book of Daniel is so early in the apocalyptic tradition that it is hard to say just what the identity of these heavenly beings are. But the larger biblical theme of a warfare that takes place in the heavenlies is seen in these early chapters of the book of Daniel and will be seen throughout the rest of the book as well. The "watchers" have been awakened, as the meaning of the Aramaic term implies, thereby now bringing judgment upon an earthly kingdom, Babylon, which has had its time of hegemony.

In Dan 5, some time has passed now taking us beyond the reign of Nebuchadnezzar to the reign of the later Babylonian ruler, Belshazzar. This will mark the end of the kingdom of Babylon, as the previous chapters in Daniel have been promising would take place. This is the famous "handwriting on the wall" chapter, an expression which has become popularized in secular culture as much as it has been in sacred culture. It basically means that some outcome is no longer in doubt, usually in reference to a negative consequence. In

the midst of Belshazzar's braggadocio, partying, and making a public spectacle of vessels captured from the Jerusalem temple, he
suddenly sees the fingers of a man's detached hand, humorously
after the fashion of "thing," from the old *Adam's Family* show,
writing a mysterious message on the wall. The transliterated Aramaic memo says, "mene, mene, tekel, upharsin" (Dan 5:25). This
cryptic message is consistent with the interpretation of the statue
dream of ch.2, where the metals are getting cheaper as one looks
from head to toe down the statue. The Aramaic cryptogram has
been interpreted by commentators in a variety of ways because of
clever wordplays and so forth, but what seems to be consistent
thought is the notion that Belshazzar's kingdom has been measured
out and is found to be lacking and his days are numbered. The
destroyed statue of ch.2, the felled tree of ch.4, and now the supernatural handwriting on the wall are all speaking the same message
– the end of earthly kingdoms is coming, and Babylon is the first to
go. The fact that Babylon meets its end in ch.5 where the handwriting incident occurs, is spelling it out with surety, just as the bible in
a number of places speaks of writing things down so as to establish
the veracity of the spoken word (e.g. Jer 36:2; Ezek 24:2; Hab 2:2;
Rev 1:11, 19). Dreams are one thing, but once things begin to get
written down, especially in ancient cultures, one can count on it
happening, in a manner of "so let it be written, so let it be done."[45]
Whereas Moses had once upon a time received the 10 commandments by the finger of God (Exod 31:15), Belshazzar now receives
this powerful judgment by the finger of God.

The apocalyptic section of Daniel, chs.7-12, will introduce us to
a variety of beasts and creatures in Daniel's dreams and visions,
some of which are unidentifiable and mysterious in human terms,
but most of which are natural creatures of the earth, such as: lions,
bears, leopards, rams, and goats. In ch.7, Daniel has a dream of his
own, which begins with him seeing four great beasts coming up
from the sea, typically representing chaos in Israelite thought,

which has been stirred up by the winds of heaven (Dan 7:2-3). The first of these beasts is a lion, which probably not coincidentally is associated with what took place in the previous chapter where the mouth of the lions were shut up when Daniel was thrown into a den of the ferocious man-eating, large cats (Dan 6:22). The question asked by the king " . . . has your God . . . been able to deliver you from the lions?" (Dan 6:20) is responded to by Daniel with "My God . . . shut the lions' mouths" (Dan 6:22), a dialogue which has strong political overtones about earthly kingdoms, represented by beasts such as lions not being able to overpower the servants of God. Paul perhaps has this in mind in his final canonical correspondence recorded in 2 Tim 4:17 in response to Nero's Rome with the declaration " . . . I was delivered out of the lion's mouth."

Though Dan 7 opens the second half of the book it still is connected to the first part of the book in that the Aramaic section which began at 2:4 continues right through chapter 7 and is completed there. Also, the dream and theme of ch.7 is parallel to the dream and theme of ch.2, although the recipients of the dreams are different (Nebuchadnezzar in ch.2 and Daniel in ch.7). This entire section, Dan 2-7, is really the nucleus of the book, with chs.8-12 being somewhat of an addendum with a more narrow focus in mind.[46] Dan 2 and 7 are especially important in that they provide the most detailed panorama of history along with a presentation of four kingdoms represented by the metals of the statue of ch.2 and the beasts which come out of the sea in ch.7. Again, these beasts have the appearance of a lion, bear, leopard, and an inexplicable terrifying beast. The lion, bear, and leopard are recognizable animals and almost certainly reflect the kingdoms of Babylon, Persia, and Alexander's Greece respectively, kingdoms that would have been identifiable to Jews any time after the 3rd century BCE. To the lion is given a human mind (Dan 7:4), similar to the experience of Nebuchadnezzar in Dan 4:34. The four wings and four heads of the leopard are consistent as imagery of the division of Alexander's

empire being divided into four quadrants after his premature death
(Dan 7:6). The devouring bear in between these two beasts would
logically fit as the Persian empire, known for its vast expansion of
territory, even as the bear in the vision is consuming meat and is
poised for further consumption (Dan 7:5). However, the fourth
beast is superlative in description (Dan 7:7). What may be more
striking is the anonymity of the creature, which Daniel is unable to
categorize in human terms like he did with the kingdoms represented by a lion, a bear, and a leopard. The beast is clearly different,
and for that matter, clearly frightening in a way that the more
recognizable beasts were not. Out of this iron-teethed, ten-horned
monster surfaces a single horn, which indicates power, resembling
a very arrogant human being (Dan 7:8, 11). To place the occasion
of this writing in the 2nd century BCE during the Jewish war with
Antiochus IV and to associate the little horn with him, would,
although not to be a foregone conclusion, certainly make sense.
However, it is possible that the Roman Empire is envisaged here
instead. Whatever the case may be, the encouraging word to the
first Jewish audience was that this little horn was going to meet its
match and be destroyed (Dan 7:11).

As Daniel is witnessing this great vision he sees two other beings come to the forefront. The first he calls the "Ancient of Days"
(Dan 7:9) and the second he calls "one like a Son of Man" (Dan
7:13). The Ancient of Days takes his seat on a throne and is described with dazzling appearance and is poised to be the judge of
the earthly events involving the beasts (Dan 7:9-10). The Son of
Man is presented before him to be a true ruler over all the earth and
the one who will serve as the antidote to the little horn (Dan 7:13-
14). The language that Daniel has used to describe this vision is of
course theologically suggestive. Earthly kingdoms and the rulers of
such kingdoms are portrayed in beastly terms. This is the worst of
humanity. Juxtaposed to this is the Son Man who is presented in an
opposite fashion as the one who characterizes what humanity

should be, namely, he is able to take his stand before the Ancient of Days and be presented before him in a way in which he is worthy to lead the peoples of the earth. As far as the phrase "Ancient of Days" goes, it is consistent with the difficulty in attempting to describe God. It is a phrase found only here in the bible, and Daniel has used it as a title of respect for the judge of all who has great wisdom and no boundaries of time. The conclusion of the Aramaic section at the end of chapter 7 could very well serve as the ending point of the book of Daniel. However, chs.8-12 will focus more on what has already been said in the book, and there will be a few other mysterious beings introduced as well.

To start with in chapter 8, Daniel records another vision subsequent to the one he had in chapter 7. Whereas the four beasts in the previous vision were wild animals, in this dream, he has a vision of animals that come from the flock, a ram and a goat to be specific. They are locked in a struggle in which the goat prevails. The interpretation is provided in vv.20-21; the ram with its two horns represents the kings of Media and Persia, with the longer horn being Persia. The goat with its large horn represents Alexander's Greek empire. The horn is quickly broken however and is replaced by four horns (Dan 8:8, 22). Out of this a king will arise who will cause great trouble before being defeated (Dan 8:23-26). This entire vision moves past the hegemony of the Babylonian empire and more narrowly focuses on the two to follow, Persia (and Media) and Greece. It is consistent with the broader focus of chapter 7 which envisions terror beyond Babylon, Persia, and the Greece of Alexander the Great. If scholars are correct in placing these texts in the book of Daniel against the backdrop of the rise of Antiochus Epiphanes in the 2nd century BCE, then we have a clear word of warning and encouragement for the oppressed Jewish peoples of this time period.

Curiously, Daniel is not alone in what he is seeing. He overhears a conversation about the matter taking place between two "holy ones (Dan 8:13)," a reminder of Nebuchadnezzar's tree dream and the words of the "watchers" there (Dan 4:13, 17, 23). Others get involved in the conversation, one of whom is identified as looking "like a man" (Dan 8:15) and another being who is identified as "Gabriel" (Dan 8:16). There is more of this in the remainder of the book of Daniel. Gabriel is mentioned again (Dan 9:21) as is a "certain man" (Dan 10:5) who most definitely is not just an ordinary human being according to the elaborate description which frightened Daniel and his companions (Dan 10:5-9, 16). This type of vision anticipates what John sees on the island of Patmos as recorded in the first chapter of the book of Revelation, of which we shall visit shortly. The stunning being speaks to Daniel about a heavenly conflict taking place which involves "the prince of the kingdom of Persia" withstanding him, but "Michael, one of the chief princes" came to help (Dan 10:13). Greece has its own prince even as Persia does (Dan 10:20). Michael appears to be a prince for Israel (Dan 10:21). The final chapter of the book of Daniel opens with this same Michael arising to take action to give the people of God final victory over all oppression and evil (Dan 12:1). These beings in the latter portion of Daniel are not clearly identified, although Gabriel and Michael are identified in larger tradition as angels. This is the only place in the Old Testament where angels are actually named, but it is from the New Testament that we know of Gabriel as an angel who "stands in the presence of God" (Lk 1:19, 26), and of Michael who is described as an "archangel" (Jd v.9; Rev 12:7).

In sum, the book of Daniel by way of organization can be further broken down from its two part structure, i.e. narrative (chs.1-6) and apocalyptic (chs.7-12), into sub-sections. Chapter one lays the foundation for the entire book by describing Daniel's obedience to God in the midst of exile and oppressive circumstances. His action here is to be the paradigm for all the faithful. Chapters 2-5 concern the fate of Babylon, although larger world history and empires are envisioned in the dream of the cheapening metals on the statue. The lion's den story of ch.6 is beyond Daniel escaping death, but rather speaks more largely to the failure of the Persian Empire to have victory over God's elect while the tamed lion speaks to what is to follow regarding the images of beasts, including a lion, in the dreams of chs.7-8. The more narrow focus of chs.7-8 is on the kingdom of Greece beyond Alexander the Great and pointing to what history would demonstrate to be the terror of Antiochus IV. This gets its most detailed attention in ch.11, with many specifics that can leave the interpreter rather bewildered. It is of course possible that Rome is imagined in all of this as well. It might be then that chs.9-10 is parenthetical, emphasizing prayer and spiritual warfare in the midst of all the conquering kingdoms and the flow of history. The final chapter of the book of Daniel, ch.12, is a short conclusion to the book. Daniel observes two more supernatural beings, described as men, having a conversation with each other and discussing all of the things that have been previously mentioned. Daniel attempts to enter the conversation with some interrogatives. He receives a response but is basically told to go his way in obedience knowing that there will be a purging, but in the end he will fare well as he stays loyal.

The book of Daniel is a powerful witness to an apocalyptic biblical theology, but the book of Revelation is the most famous of all apocalyptic writings, whether canonical or non-canonical literature. In fact, the first word of the Greek text of Revelation is Ἀποκάλυψις ("apokalypsis"), letting the reader know that this is specifically a revelation of Jesus Christ. This book is often times simply called "the Apocalypse." The Greek verbal definition of the term is "to reveal," as in the opening up of understanding into the spatial and temporal elements of the invisible world and of linear time that human beings do not normally see into with natural eyes. Many of the types of beasts and creatures that appear in Daniel appear in Revelation as well. One distinct difference is that at this

point in the tradition of the Jews and Christians Satan has now
taken a leading role in the cosmic campaign and conflict with God.
An outbreak of Satanic activity is envisioned.[47] The historic occasion of the writing of Revelation has changed of course from the
background of the writing of Daniel. Whereas Daniel is placed
somewhere between the rule of Babylon and the Syrian-Greek rule
of Antiochus IV, Revelation is placed at the end of the first century
CE, when Rome had its rule under emperor Domitian.

The initial vision of Christ given to John on the island of Patmos
has amazing similarities to Daniel's encounter with "a certain man"
(Dan 10:5-10). Besides the physical description that is so akin, the
surrendered and paralyzed response of John and the hand touch of
the heavenly being also resonates Daniel's experience. Even the
"Ancient of Days" of Dan 7:9-10 bears resemblance. This opening
vision lays the foundation for the remainder of the book in that all
that takes place is to be interpreted through the lens of who Christ is
in his amazing glorified and apocalyptic state. After Christ gives
customized edicts to the seven churches of western Asia Minor
(chs.2-3) in the fashion of the true emperor, juxtaposed to Domitian's Rome, the open door in heaven (Rev 4:1) is an invitation to
look into the realm of the spatial and invisible battle taking place
between God and the forces of evil. The seven churches Jesus
addresses might not look like much compared to the vast Roman
Empire which expands across the Mediterranean basin, but as heav-
en is opened up in chapters 4-5 with all of its vast and impressive
scenery, one begins to get the idea that Jesus really is the true
emperor over a great kingdom such as the book of Daniel envisioned.

The images that John records for his audience include not only
an open door in heaven, but a throne that is central to the entirety of
the vision. It is, not surprisingly, described in elaborate terms as we
have seen in Old Testament throne room visions, and it includes a
variety of creatures and beings not to dissimilar to what Isaiah and

Ezekiel witnessed (Rev 4:6-8). It also includes twenty-four elders sitting on thrones of their own. And although these elders remain unexplained, they are probably best understood with representing the twelve tribes of Israel and the twelve apostles of Jesus and their witness to the truth of God across the span of both Old and New Testaments. All the beings and creatures in the heavenly throne room worship the one who sits on the throne, but what is going to attract John is that the one who sits on this throne, God no doubt, holds a sealed up book in his hand, and there is no one within the expanse of all creation worthy to take the book, break it open, and reveal its contents. A "strong angel" makes a loud public inquiry in search of one who might be counted worthy to take the document and open it up, but the initial search is unsuccessful (Rev 5:2-3). John desperately wants to know what the book says, so much so that he begins to weep because it remains sealed. The vision can go no further unless someone can break open the seals, probably of a scroll, and allow for the contents to be seen. In the course of every-day life today one may be frustrated by not being able to open a package, a can, or a bottle, but this is big; it has cosmic ramifications.

But then one of the elders speaks to John, informing him that the search has ended with success. The contents of the document can be revealed. This worthy one who has been found is characterized as a "lion, that is from the tribe of Judah, the Root of David," all of which are messianic descriptions (Rev 5:5). Yet what is rather startling is that this "lion" turns out to be a "lamb," and a slain one at that (Rev 5:6). The antithetical nature of the two creatures can hardly be missed. One is a wild beast, "king of the forest," and the first of the creatures in Daniel's vision of Daniel chapter seven representing human empires. But a lamb is the most passive of animals from the flock and to exacerbate matters even more; this is one that has already been offered up sacrificially. This one who has the strength, power, and ferocity of a lion can also act as a passive lamb, and herein lays the mystery of the Christian Gospel and its paradoxical nature. In the book of Daniel and also soon to be seen in the book of Revelation there are numerous apocalyptic beasts and creatures which represent humankind in its worst imaginable forms as well as enemies of God in the invisible world. But the one who will conquer all of these human and non-human beasts is the least intimidating of all creatures, a lamb that has been slain. It is an incredible coup d'état.

The lamb dares to go where no one else can go. He boldly walks right up to the throne and takes the book out of the hand of the one who sits on the throne (Rev 5:7). An incredible response of worship follows as all the heavenly beings, including a multitude of angels, fall down before the lamb playing music, singing songs, offering incense, prayers, and declarations of the purchase of humanity that the lamb bought for God with his own blood. The heavenly host which sang "worthy" to the one who sat on the throne (Rev 4:11) now also sing "worthy" to the lamb for his sacrificial death and his purchase of humanity (Rev 5:9, 12).

Chapters 4-5 in the book of Revelation have brought John into a sort of cosmic showroom. The one who sits on the throne and the slain lamb will be central to all the activity he will witness through-out the remainder of the book. The heavenly host of angels, elders, and living creatures will also feature predominately throughout the book. But now that the lamb has the scroll it can be opened so that the contents can be revealed, and the contents are of course the record of Rev 6-22. The first of the seven seals is broken and the four proverbial horseman of the apocalypse begin to be revealed one by one as each of the first four seals is broken in successive order. There were shadows of this sort of apocalyptic flavor back in the book of Zechariah (Zech 1:8-17; 6:1-8). With the first seal comes a rider on a white horse, indicating war and conquest. The second rider rides a red horse, which is the color of bloodshed as a result of the sword and warfare brought by the first rider. Rider number three gallops on a black horse, this being a portrait of scarcity, inflation, price gauging, and famine. The last rider trots on a pale, or ashen horse, the color of illness, disease, and death.

Keeping historic context in mind, the terror that Emperor Domitian brought is certainly being characterized by the four horseman of the apocalypse. The opening of the fifth seal shows that indeed some of the faithful have been martyred by the events happening on earth, but they are now safely waiting for God to bring final justice. The opening of the sixth seal reveals further cosmic upheaval and universal calamity which is then followed by a strange calm before a further storm which sets apart the people of God during this time of great trial and tribulation (Rev 7).

The opening of the seventh seal, which now brings us to Rev 8, begins with silence in heaven for half an hour. It is a further eerie calm and silence before the impending storm that the seventh seal brings. Then the silence is broken by seven angels blowing seven trumpets, quite a contrast from a moment of silence. The trumpet blasts bring warning concerning a devastated earth which is plagued in a manner even greater than what was witnessed in Egypt back in the days of Moses. There are similarities, such as water turning to blood and darkness. Things are so bad after trumpet four that a bird of some sort, probably a carrion bird because of the massive amount of corpses lying around, is flying through midheaven announcing how bad it is yet going to get as a result of the remaining three trumpet blasts. Up to this point the natural created order has been attacked, but now, humans will directly take the brunt of the judgment.

With the fifth trumpet blast the bottomless pit is opened and a plague of locust is unleashed. This is also reminiscent of the Egyptian plagues; however, these locusts are quite different and described as ferocious, terrifying, and even other worldly (Rev 9:3-10). The Greek god Apollo was symbolized by the locust, and it may be that Domitian, who claimed to be an incarnation of Apollo, is being characterized as the leader of this locust pack from hell (Rev 9:11). We are not told the number of locust, but we are told the number of horseman that ride as a conquering army when the sixth seal is opened—two hundred million (Rev 9:16). They too get an elaborate description, with features of that of the lion and serpent, creatures which figured in Daniel and here in Revelation. There is also a hint of the Genesis 3 snake. The origin of this army from the region of the Euphrates is a reminder of past armies who have marched west from that vicinity, including the Assyrians, the Babylonians, and even the potential threat to the present Roman Empire, the Parthian hordes. There is a sense here that much of history is in view with John's vision in that distant resonances to the plagues of Egypt, allusions to the ancient Mesopotamian invasions from beyond the Euphrates—Assyria, Babylon, the mentioning of the Greek name Apollyon (Rev 9:11), and of course the more obvious concern of the present occupation of Rome, are all contained within this great apocalyptic vision.

This type of apocalyptic literature in the book of Revelation requires more imagination than it does analyzation in matters of interpretation. At this point of the revelation to John, all seven seals have been opened and six of the seven trumpets of the last seal have sounded. As far as mysterious beasts and creatures go, we have seen the four horseman of the apocalypse, as well as a strange locust plague and an invasion of a numerous army of horseman from the east. One thing is clear, the seven churches of Asia Minor that are being addressed in this book will know that a tremendous time of turmoil is coming upon planet earth, indicated by the heavenly scene John has been witnessing. Just as there was an interlude with the breaking of the seventh seal so also there is an interlude with the blowing of the seventh trumpet. The seventh item, be it a seal or a trumpet, are acting as a final, climactic occurrence of the larger whole. Before the seventh trumpet is sounded there is a "strong angel" holding a "little book" which had been opened (Rev

10:1-2). It is not clear if this is the same book that was bound by the seven seals or even if the strong angel is Jesus himself. But what happens next is curious. John is told by a heavenly voice to go and take the book from the angel, and when the angel gives him the book he tells him he must eat the scroll (Rev 10:8-9). This is patterned after the prophet Ezekiel (Ezek 2:8-3:3) with the one caveat that although John would taste sweetness in the scroll as Ezekiel had, he would experience bitterness in his stomach, unlike Ezekiel. Ezekiel's visions were of course very foreboding in his context but it appears that for John's day things will be even worse.

Finally, the seventh trumpet sounds and there is great fanfare in heaven concerning the shaking up of heaven and earth and the turning over of all earthly kingdoms to Christ the Lord (Rev 11:15-19). A late term pregnant woman clothed with the sun and moon and wearing a crown of twelve stars on her head appears in the vision and she is being pursued by a dragon who desires to devour her child when born (Rev 12:1-4). Most certainly the woman represents the people of God and the child who is born is Christ, who according to the vision ascends to God, as the Gospels tell us about Jesus. As for the woman, she is still on earth and has to flee for her life from the dragon, but she has a safe hiding place prepared by God (Rev 12:6). Then the scene switches from earth to the heavenlies, where there is a war taking place involving the Michael whom we know from the book of Daniel, and the dragon. We also learn that both Michael and the dragon have their own contingencies of angels who are involved in the cosmic combat (Rev12:7). This is really big! It is universal in scale and it all revolves around the woman and her male child. Christ and his people is so much the object of the conflict. The dragon is fighting a losing battle and this creature is further identified as " . . . the serpent of old who is called the devil and Satan . . . " (Rev 12:9). With this passage we have the embodiment of evil all rolled up into one since the first obscure reference to this being as a serpent in the Garden of Eden in Gene-

sis 3 right on through the few "Satan" passages in the Old Testament and the many "Satan" and "devil" passages in the New Testament. This is climactic for this dragon, and he receives much attention throughout the remainder of Revelation 12 in regards to his
intense hatred and contempt for the woman and her child. The
dragon will experience a three - fold progressive falling in the book
of Revelation, starting with this chapter where he falls from heaven
to earth (Rev 12:9), and then falls again from the earth to the abyss
(Rev 20:2-3), and then one more time, falling from the abyss to the
lake of fire (Rev 20:10). It is complete reversal and irony from the
beginning of the biblical story when the serpent led humans to fall
from God in the temptation story of Genesis 3.

The introduction of Michael the archangel into the drama has
brought to mind the apocalyptic elements in the book of Daniel.
This continues on into the thirteenth chapter of the book of Revelation where two beasts rise up, one from the sea (Rev 13:1) and one
from the earth (Rev 13:11). The sea beast is like the beasts of
Daniel 7, but the order is reversed: leopard, bear, and lion. Also,
this beast speaks arrogant words (Rev 13:5) after the fashion of the
horn in Daniel 7 which in that context would have more than likely
referred to Antiochus IV. The combination of the dragon and the
two beasts strive for the religious allegiance of the entire world,
perhaps representing Roman cultic priests, magicians, astrologers
and any other entities that would have fostered pagan emperor worship in the context of the late first century CE. Whether the empire
is led by Antiochus, Domitian, or any other dominant world leader,
the point is clear that the lamb will ultimately defeat all these op-
pressors and dictators and that those who remain faithful to the
lamb will be overcomers with him. This in essence is the book of
Revelation. The two beasts that arose in chapter thirteen, one from
the sea and one from the land, bring us back to our Old Testament
understanding of all that Leviathan and Behemoth would have represented in the imagery and mythology of the ancient world. In

fact, as part of the final vision of the book of Revelation John sees that in the new heaven and new earth there is no longer any sea (Rev 21:1). This may be a coded way of saying that all chaos and evil are all gone, seeing that the sea was representative of what humans feared and was bad. The lack of a sea would certainly be the undoing of Leviathan, thereby letting the reader know that indeed all that is wrong in the world is now done away with in God's new kingdom. The destruction of beasts, false prophets, and the one known as "dragon, serpent, devil, Satan" as recorded in the previous chapter (i.e. Rev 20) has already driven home this point. There are of course other mysterious creatures mentioned between Revelation chapter thirteen and Revelation chapter twenty, such as "unclean spirits like frogs" (Rev 16:13), "spirits of demons" (Rev 16:14), and a "harlot woman" indicative of Rome (Rev 17), but the destruction of the dragon and his minions, along with Leviathan by implication, provides the final clue to God's victory over all evil in the world.

SUMMARY

Although Leviathan is mentioned in the bible only a handful of times, the impact of the creature has been fairly far reaching in popular culture. For instance, Thomas Hobbes' well known book published in 1651, which is entitled *Leviathan*, used the image of the giant sea creature during the time of the English civil war to critique societal structure and government legitimacy. His social and political world had become a Leviathan, so to speak. Also, the American poet George Oppen entitled his 1962 poem *Leviathan* to speak on a larger scale to the impact of all of humankind's actions. For him, everything we humans do becomes an all-consuming force, a Leviathan, ready to destroy and devour. More recently, a 2014 movie was named *Leviathan*, which featured a common Russian man living on a coastal town who was fighting governmental forces to keep his home. This is just a small sampling of the kinds of works of art and human endeavors which have played off of the Old Testament feared creature of the deep and what it represents. Leviathan then, has become in popular culture a codified way of speaking about forces which become overwhelming and dangerous for the human situation. The monster of the deep from the bible is therefore one of the most familiar ways to express concern for forces which seem well beyond our control. For Old Testament Israel, and especially the prophet Isaiah, Leviathan represented the sum of all of Israel's enemies. The use of Leviathan in popular culture in the modern world is thereby probably a good and useful way to get a strong point across.

Although we have in the bible a specific sea creature with a specific name, Leviathan, that represents terror and evil, the bible still has other ways of expressing the Leviathan concept. That is, there are Leviathan type creatures which make biblical appearances to reinforce the Leviathan concept, not least of which is the serpent, who comes on the scene early in the biblical narrative (Gen 3). Along with serpents, there are sea monsters as well who are not named Leviathan, one such example being "Rahab," who most typically represents the power of the Egyptians in the Old Testament period. In fact, such sea monsters, including Leviathan, are pretty much to be associated with empires and leaders who pose a threat to the stability of the world and especially smaller nations like Israel. Rahab, like Leviathan, is ultimately defeated by Yahweh. So also, serpents and cognate type creatures are defeated in the administration of Jesus as is seen by his teaching of his disciples that they would "tread upon serpents and all the power of the enemy (Lk.10:19)." Leviathan not only has colleague sea creatures, but there is also the associated land creature known as "Behemoth" mentioned in the world of the Old Testament. If Leviathan represents all the chaos, terror, and fear of the deep waters and the mystery of such, Behemoth represents everything else in the world that is feared and troubling. These two together are a tandem to speak to evil in the world, which can be found everywhere. They may belong to the natural world, that is within the literal animal kingdom, such as whales, rhinos, and the hippo. But they more so belong to the supernatural world and the element of ancient myth that they embody.

The development of apocalyptic literature late in the Old Testament period introduced more types of mysterious beasts and creatures into biblical theology. Glimpses of this can be seen in the writings of the prophets Isaiah and Ezekiel, who give us insight into the heavenly realm and even the throne room of God to depict that there are other worldly forces at work in a larger cosmic campaign to combat evil. The foremost apocalypses in the bible are of course Daniel in the Old Testament and Revelation in the New Testament. In Daniel, Nebuchadnezzar's dreams of the statue and tree, both of which are cut down by external and even heavenly forces, serve to teach of the eventual collapse of all human empires and the appearance of the kingdom of God. Human kings and kingdoms are depicted as beasts, but they will all be destroyed in a larger, heavenly warfare which also introduces God as "the ancient of days" and "one like a son of man." Although the book of Daniel has diversity regarding which human empires are envisioned (i.e. Babylon, Persian, Greece, etc.), the book of Revelation has distinctively the rule of the Roman Empire as the context of the writing of the book. Revelation chapters 4-5 bring the reader into the heavenly throne room in a manner similar to Isaiah and Ezekiel, but with even a greater sense of pageantry and demonstration. This is the true Emperor's palace, far exceeding the boast of Roman Caesars. The lion who is also paradoxically a slain lamb takes center stage in the drama and begins to break open the book which reveals the ultimate defeat of not only Rome, but Satan himself, who is also called on more than one occasion a "dragon, serpent, and the devil." The beasts and creatures that appear in the book of Revelation have many similarities with the beasts and creatures that appear in the book of Daniel. However, in the book of Revelation, Satan features predominately and he and his beasts are defeated once and for all by God and his divine forces. In the end, there is no more sea and seemingly no more place for Leviathan to swim about freely. That is, once and for all, all evil, moral and otherwise is gone for good in God's new kingdom. Leviathan is under control.

NOTES

1. Clements, *Isaiah 1-39*, p.218.

2. NRSV.

3. L. McFall, *New Dictionary of Biblical Theology*, p.774.

4. Ibid., p.774.

5. J.H. Walton, *Dictionary of the Old Testament Pentateuch* (T. Desmond Alexander & David W. Baker, Ed.) (Downers Grove, Ill., Leicester, England: InterVarsity Press, 2003), p.737.

6. Ibid., p.738.

7. Clements, *Isaiah 1-39*, p.218.

8. Gray, *Isaiah I-XXVII*, p.449.

9. Seitz, *Isaiah 1-39*, p.198.

10. Watts, *Isaiah 1-33*, p.348.

11. Gray, *Isaiah I-XXVII*, p.450.

12. Oswalt, *The Book of Isaiah*, p.491.

13. Robert S. Fyall, *Now my Eyes have seen You: Images of creation and evil in the book of Job* (New Studies in Biblical Theology, D.A. Carson, Ed.) (Downers Grove, Ill.: InterVarsity Press, 2002), p.171.

14. Ibid., p.171.

15. Oswalt, *The Book of Isaiah*, p.491.

16. Goldingay, *The Theology of the Book of Isaiah*, p.47.

17. Fyall, *Now my Eyes have seen You*, p.170.

18. In the Christian Bible, whereas in the Hebrew Bible it is Job 40:25.

19. Ibid., p.157.

20. Elmer B. Smick, *Job (The Expositor's Bible Commentary)* (Frank E. Gaebelein, Gen. Ed., vol.4) (Grand Rapids, Mi.: Zondervan, 1988), p.1051.

21. Fyall, *Now my Eyes have seen You*, p.127.

22. Ibid., pp.126-137.

23. Oswalt, *The Book of Isaiah*, p.548.

24. Joyce G. Baldwin, *Daniel: An Introduction & Commentary* (Tyndale Old Testament Commentaries, D.J. Wiseman, Gen. Ed.) (Downers Grove, Ill.: InterVarsity Press, 1978), p.47.

25. Stanley J. Grenz, David Guretzki & Cherith Fee Nordling, *Pocket Dictionary of Theological Terms* (Downers Grove, Ill.: InterVarsity Press, 1999), p.13.

26. Leon Morris, *Revelation* (Tyndale New Testament Commentaries, Revised Edition) (Leicester, England: InterVarsity Press, 1992), p.24.

27. Baldwin, *Daniel*, p.54.

28. Ibid., p.50.

29. Morris, *Revelation*, p.24.

30. Grenz, Guretzki & Cherith, *Pocket Dictionary of Theological Terms*, p.13.

31. Baldwin, *Daniel*, p.54.

32. Berlin and Brettler, *The Jewish Study Bible Tanakh Translation*, p.1046.

33. William H. Brownlee, *Ezekiel 1-19* (Word Biblical Commentary) (Waco, Tx.: Word Books, 1986), p.11.

34. Ralph W. Klein, *Ezekiel: The Prophet and His Message* (Columbia, S.C.: University of South Carolina Press, 1988), p.25.

35. Ibid., p.11.

36. Brownlee, *Ezekiel 1-19*, p.12.

37. Clements, *Isaiah 1-39*, p.74.

38. Ibid., p.74.

39. Ibid., p.74.

40. Geoffrey W. Grogan, *Isaiah (The Expositor's Bible Commentary)* (Frank E. Gaebelein, Gen. Ed., vol.6) (Grand Rapids, Mi.: Zondervan, 1986), p.55.

41. Ibid., p.55.

42. Baldwin, *Daniel*, p.47.

43. Ibid., p.49.

44. This fourth man, who is one as "a son of the gods" is often taken in popular Christian interpretation as an appearance of the pre-incarnate Christ. Most of biblical scholarship however would not adopt this view, but would see it as a statement of Nebuchadnezzar's paganistic world view. Nonetheless, this fourth man is some sort of supernatural mediator who serves as a glimpse of what will be seen from the heavenly realm in the apocalyptic section of Daniel which is to follow. This is not the last we will see of this in the book of Daniel.

45. A line taken from Pharaoh in Cecil B. Demil's movie *"The Ten Commandments."*

46. Baldwin, *Daniel*, p.154.

47. Morris, *Revelation*, p.26.

Chapter Three

Lilith

We began the first chapter of this book by noting that Lucifer is not a stranger to the secular world and of course, certainly is not a stranger to the religious world. Lucifer is well known. Leviathan, the topic of our second chapter, is much lesser known, although the creature does make more appearances in the bible than Lucifer and also finds its way into some pop culture as well. The topic of our third and final chapter is "Lilith." Whereas Lilith is somewhat known in secular and pop culture, she is hardly known at all in the world of the Church or Synagogue. This is understandable, as there is just a scant reference to her in the bible, and even then, she is hardly recognizable. But the mystery and intrigue behind her personage is certainly worth investigating.

LILITH INSIDE THE BIBLE

Not surprisingly, we return to the book of Isaiah to begin our investigation. Our studies of Lucifer and Leviathan began here. It is in Isa 34:14 only that the Hebrew proper noun "Lilith" makes an appearance in the bible. The passage reads, "Wildcats shall meet with hyenas, goat-demons shall call to each other; there too Lilith shall repose, and find a place to rest (NRSV)." This sole biblical reference to Lilith is contained within a larger section of judgment texts with the nation of Edom being in particular focus. Edom, because of its historical relationship and reputation with the Jews rooted in the twin brothers Esau and Jacob, might be representative here of judgment on all nations.[1] Lilith keeps company in the passage with frightful desert creatures such as jackals, ostriches, owls, wolves, goats, hawks, and snakes. For this reason, Lilith is often associated with being a night animal or some sort of nocturnal monster that is a rather allusive and mysterious being or creature. English translations verify this, although some translations keep the actual word "Lilith" in the text. Isaiah's use of the term appears to be for the purpose of capturing the imaginations of the Israelite people who would have understood the terror that Lilith could bring. We shall see in a moment that Lilith's origins are in Mesopotamian culture and folklore where she is something much more than just a bird-like animal, but is rather a creature from the world of the demonic and supernatural. The line between exotic haunting animals such as snakes, owls, jackals etc. and other-worldly phantoms, ghosts, and demons is not always clearly drawn.[2] The animal list in Isa 34:14 mentions some sort of goat which has raised speculation as to whether or not this is a literal animal or an idol or even a demon reference, as our NSRV translation has suggested. Because this creature runs parallel in the text with Lilith, it reinforces the notion that we are perhaps dealing with creatures outside of the known animal kingdom or the sphere of the natural. It is fascinating that although there is just this one biblical reference to Lilith she has gone on to have a "remarkable career"[3] outside the world of the bible. We shall turn to this in a moment. However, to a much lesser extent, Lilith has had a rather remarkable career inside the world of the bible as well because of some readers' interpretive moves, mostly as a result of her later fame outside the bible.

The later legends of Lilith that we shall be discussing momentarily has influenced some bible readers to see her making an appearance on God's grand stage in the opening narratives of the book of Genesis. It is a sort of folk theology using eisegesis and later medieval Jewish mythical theology that reads between the lines in the creation of humans spoken of in Gen 1:26-29; 2:4-8; 2:21-25; and 5:1-2. It has similarities with the so-called "gap theory" which hypothesizes a large period of time between Gen 1:1 and Gen 1:2 where God had supposedly created a first race of human beings, "pre-Adamic" so to speak, who sinned greatly against God and were destroyed before starting over with Adam. The similar Lilith legend contends that Lilith was created before Eve and was Adam's first wife, a spouse from which Adam became estranged. The legend goes along the lines of believing that Gen.1:26-29 speaks of Adam and Lilith being first created, but Lilith is not created in God's image in the manner of Adam. Gen 2:4-8 supposedly also speaks to Adam and Lilith being in the world as the first human couple with Lilith being represented by the mist that came up from the ground in v.6. It is mystical interpretation. A straightforward reading of the text most certainly does not lend to this interpretation and some extreme eisegesis becomes necessary to take this view. It goes on to hypothesize that Gen 2:21-25 is bringing Eve into the story for the first time as a sort of replacement for the relationship gone bad between Adam and his first wife Lilith. Proponents of the Lilith in Genesis theory understand the statement of Gen 2:18 " . . . it is not good for the man to be alone . . . " to mean that Adam "became alone," thereby suggesting that his first wife left him. Adam's positive response therefore in Gen 2:23 is because although Lilith was a failure, Eve will be an improvement because she has come from his own body. But this seems to go quite obviously against the grain of the text which is demonstrating that the animals God created were not sufficient to meet Adam's needs (Gen 2:20). Eve, to be named later on (Gen 3:20), is most certainly Adam's first and only wife, as the larger tradition has passed on without much debate or contradiction. But the Lilith legend purports that Lilith indeed became the very serpent that tempted Eve in the garden out of her own jealousy, and was successful because she perhaps ate the forbidden fruit herself in the presence of Eve without suffering any immediate consequence, thereby convincing Eve to partake.

A better and more natural reading of the text is to understand Gen 1:26-29 as a grand pronouncement of God's great plan to bring humans into the world as those beings which are his very image. There is no concern yet for an Adam or an Eve, and certainly not for a Lilith. It is the climax of all he has done in the creation week. It is more a telescopic view of God's great design for the heavens and earth – humans are created! Gen 2 is then a more microscopic look at the specifics of humans, the grandest creatures of all God's creative work. Adam is first focused upon (Gen 2:4-8) to be followed by a focus on the woman – Eve (Gen 2:21-25). Gen 5:1-2 is a recap of the creation of the first human couple, Adam and Eve, and serves as a kind of end parenthesis, even as Gen 1:26-27, using similar language, is a kind of beginning parenthesis. In sum, the creation of humans mentioned in Gen 1 & 5 are broad statements of the blessing and likeness to God of humans whereas the specifics of Gen 2 are for the purpose of detailing out how both the first man and the first woman came into existence and how they would become united. There is no mention of Lilith here, and there is no place for trying to fit her sublimely into the storyline. But as we shall see, her place in the Genesis narrative by some will come about much later because of her fame that would develop in subsequent Jewish thought. Lilith would then be superimposed back on the Genesis text to come up with the rather strange interpretation that we have provided in brief. The way this happened will be seen in our exploration of Lilith in the world outside of the bible. However, within the bible, Lilith is only mentioned one time with any degree of certainty. And that is of course within Isa 34:14, where

Lilith finds herself part of a list of frightening and haunting desert creatures.

LILITH OUTSIDE THE BIBLE

The first known literary reference to Lilith exists outside the bible and pre-dates Isaiah by more than a millennium. It is found in the famed Epic of Gilgamesh from Mesopotamian literature, being specifically, a Sumerian tale known as "Gilgamesh and the Huluppu Tree." It dates as far back as circa 2000 BCE. There has been, as one might expect, a certain amount of scholarly discussion around the identity of this Lilith and her association with Isaiah's Lilith.[4] In the tale, the goddess Inanna walks about a garden of the gods with a desire to approach a Huluppu tree which she eventually wants to use to make a chair and a couch. On the top of the tree sits a bird and at the base of the tree a snake makes its nest. Also, "Lilith," who is referred to as "a maid of desolation," makes herself a home in the middle of the tree. The bird, the snake, and Lilith create fear in Inanna, who is unable to approach the tree to claim her eventual furniture prize. Thankfully for her, the hero Gilgamesh intervenes to kill the snake and forces the bird and Lilith to flee from the tree. Inanna is able to then go and take the tree for her purposes. The similar themes of serpents, sacred trees, and gardens between the story of Gilgamesh and the Huluppu Tree and the biblical Eden story of Gen 3 are rather obvious. Lilith's presence at the Huluppu Tree gives some, albeit very little, ammunition for those who want to see her in early Genesis. As we shall see in the later Jewish literature to be discussed, Lilith becomes one with the serpent in Gen 3 and also will be known for her bird-like quality of being able to fly away. Does this mean that we should read between the lines in Gen 1-5 to see Lilith there? I would contend "no," for it would require more eisegesis than it would exegesis to make that interpretive move and would allow mystical interpretation to dominate thereby dismissing any hermeneutical control of how the text is read.

Anyhow, the Epic of Gilgamesh is not the only place where a Lilith theme makes an appearance in the Ancient Near East. The clay artifact originally known as the "Burney Relief," named for its first owner in 1936 and now referred to as the "Lilith Relief" and is housed in the British Museum dates back to roughly 2000 BCE, close to the origin of the Gilgamesh Epic. There is a central figure in the clay artwork whose identity is contested, with some support for Lilith as the subject. Also, the "Nippur bowls" come from ancient Babylonia and demonstrate that the Lilith legend had influence at the time of their production, dating much later to circa 600 CE. Twenty-six out of forty of these incantation bowls mention Lilith in attempts to ward off diseases and demons. These come from a Jewish colony in existence in that part of the world due to the diaspora and they reveal that the Lilith legend was alive and well in the folklore of common Jewish people by the early Middle Ages. One such inscription on an incantation bowl reads "The evil Lilith . . . causes the hearts of men to go astray and appears in the dreams of the night and in the vision of the day, who burns and casts down with nightmare, attacks and kills children . . . " Amulets from the millennium to follow have also been discovered from that part of the world. The evidence shows that Jewish women placed these amulets above the bed or on the wall during childbirth for the purpose of warding off Lilith. A Kabbalistic work from circa 1100 CE known as the "Book of Raziel" refers to Lilith in an amulet as "primitive Eve," which portrays her as a child slayer in the manner of the Nippur bowls. Even the Babylonian Talmud, produced by Jewish communities of the diaspora for the purpose of preserving ancient knowledge, has a handful of brief references to Lilith. This work of about 400 CE demonstrates that educated and sophisticated Jews preserved the Lilith legend as much as more simplistic Jews of the incantation and amulet variety. In brief, the Talmud's five or so references to Lilith reveal that she was believed to be contemporary with Adam and responsible for stealing his seed by which she would sire demon children and then go on to defile other women in childbirth. Her physical description is that of having long hair and wings. Somewhat contemporary with the Talmud is a pseudepigraphical work knows as the "Testament of Solomon" (c. 200-600 CE) which has a story of a Lilith-like being who has long hair. Although there are differing versions of the story, this character goes by the alias "Obizuth" (or the alternate spelling "Obyzouth"). Such aliases were not uncommon for the Jewish literature of this period, for numerous characters in the abundance of stories went by more than one name. In the story, King Solomon is ordering demons to appear before him and this particular Obizuth/Obyzouth is to appear before the king for her crime of strangling unprotected newborn children. She is known for her disheveled hair and is ultimately bound and hung by her hair in front of the Temple as a spectacle by order of Solomon. As Samson was once known for his long hair being a symbol of strength and power, similarly for women in the ancient world, long hair could symbolize power which was associated with sexuality and seductiveness. To be hung up by the hair as Obizuth/Obyzouth was to basically be judged for crimes of promiscuity and sexual misdeeds. Lilith was of course known for being a seductress with evil intent. Lilith also seems to make a sneak appearance in the Aramaic Targum known as "Pseudo Jonathan." This work is speculated to have been written anywhere from 400-1400 CE. This particular Targum adds a prayer to the famous Aaronic blessing of Num 6:24-26 making it to read "May the Lord bless you in all your deeds and protect you from the demons of the 'night' (ליליי in Aramaic) and from anything that frightens and from demons of evening and morning, from evil spirits and phantoms". The word for "night" and "Lilith" are so similar here in the Aramaic language that it is difficult to distinguish between the two and may reinforce the notion of a plurality of female night demons that go around terrorizing young mothers and small children.

There are two late medieval Jewish writings that have more to say about Lilith than any of those already mentioned. The first is known as the "Alphabet of Ben Sira" and the second is called the "Zohar." "The Alphabet" as it is sometimes known in its shortened form was written around 800-900 CE in a Midrashim style that is full of satire, parodies, and irreverence unlike any of the Jewish works we have discussed thus far.[5] Some of its rather impertinent topics include: flatulation, urination, masturbation, and copulation. One wonders if this was penned by an anti-Jewish anarchist who sought to ridicule the religious traditions of the Jews or if it was written by a serious rabbi who sought to bring a light comedy into the mix for entertainment purposes. That is, this may have been a Jew who wrote a sort of academic burlesque with an ability to make fun of his own tradition through satire. One thing for sure, the great medieval Jewish philosopher Maimonides of Spain did not find it funny, nor did other Jewish religious teachers in regards to "the Alphabet." It puts forth that Ben Sira is the son of the prophet Jeremiah's daughter. However, oddly enough, it also purports in some editions of the story that Jeremiah is the father of Ben Sira at the same time as being his grandfather. This came about as a result of forced onanism, a term taken from the biblical story of Onan who refused to impregnate his widowed sister-in-law to fulfill a levirate responsibility (Gen 38:9). That is, Jeremiah supposedly spilled his seed outside of the vagina, but the emissions nonetheless impregnated his daughter when she came to bathe. This is especial-ly curious in light of Yahweh's mandate for Jeremiah to not marry nor to have children (Jer 16:2). "The Alphabet" tells the story of Ben Sira's conception, birth, early education, as well as his life adventures and later reflections from his own son and grandson. The name of the work results from Ben Sira's teacher attempting to teach the youngster the alphabet by which Ben Sira responds with great elaborations rather than just repeating the twenty two letter Hebrew alphabet. Lilith is not mentioned until the latter portion of the work which takes place in the court of King Nebuchadnezzar. Nebuchadnezzar sets ordeals before Ben Sira expecting him to resolve them in a fashion similar to how we see the king have high expectations for those who serve in his court as recorded in the book of Daniel. At one point, Nebuchadnezzar's son is ill and the king asks Ben Sira to heal the lad. Ben Sira responds by telling a story which involves Lilith. This has become the most quoted Lilith story today. The passage from "The Alphabet" which tells the story of Lilith is reproduced here in its entirety:

> Soon afterward the young son of the king took ill. Said Nebuchadnezzar, "Heal my son. If you don't, I will kill you." Ben Sira immediately sat down to write an amulet with the Holy Name, and he inscribed on it the angels in charge of medicine by their names, forms, and images, and by their wings, hands, and feet. Nebuchadnezzar looked at the amulet. "Who are these?"
>
> "The angels who are in charge of medicine: Snvi, Snvsi, and Smnglof. After God created Adam, who was alone, He said, 'It is not good for man to be alone' (Genesis 2:18). He then created a woman for Adam, from the earth, as He had created Adam himself, and called her Lilith. Adam and Lilith immediately began to fight. She said, 'I will not lie below,' and he said, 'I will not lie beneath you, but only on top. For you are fit only to be in the bottom position, while I am to be the superior one.' Lilith responded, 'We are equal to each other inasmuch as we were both created from the earth.' But they would not listen to one another. When Lilith saw this, she pronounced the Ineffable Name and flew away into the air. Adam stood in prayer before his Creator: 'Sovereign of the universe!' he said, 'the woman you gave me has run away.' At once, the Holy One, blessed by He, sent these three angels to bring her back."
>
> "Said the Holy One to Adam, 'If she agrees to come back, fine. If not, she must permit one hundred of her children to die every day.' The angels left God and pursued Lilith, whom they overtook in the midst of the sea, in the mighty waters wherein

the Egyptians were destined to drown. They told her God's word, but she did not wish to return. The angels said, 'We shall drown you in the sea.'"

"'Leave me!' she said. 'I was created only to cause sickness to infants. If the infant is male, I have dominion over him for eight days after his birth, and if female, for twenty days.'"

"When the angels heard Lilith's words, they insisted she go back. But she swore to them by the name of the living and eternal God: 'Whenever I see you or your names or your forms in an amulet, I will have no power over that infant.' She also agreed to have one hundred of her children die every day. Accordingly, every day one hundred demons perish, and for the same reason, we write the angels names on the amulets of young children. When Lilith sees their names, she remembers her oath, and the child recovers."[6]

In sum then, the Lilith legend in "The Alphabet of Ben Sira" accomplishes two purposes. Firstly, it provides an explanation for the two creation accounts. In Gen 1, God creates Lilith, and in Gen 2, God creates Eve. Secondly, it provides an explanation for the amulet tradition. This means of course that the story is not to be taken seriously and legends such as Lilith should be taken rather, with a grain of salt so to speak. Nonetheless, this tradition of Lilith arguing with her husband over sexual positions, then flying away from her husband only to be brought back by God for a negotiation mediated by angels that explains why some children die and why some are spared, has managed to take root not only in medieval culture, but in modern culture as well. Lilith has become this evil woman who steals semen, is immensely fertile, spawns demon children at an astronomical rate, and then seeks revenge upon human children in retaliation for the daily deaths of her demonic offspring. She also has become the negative role model, at least from the standpoint of patriarchy, of the non-submissive wife who argues with her husband and tries to usurp authority over him. A more feminist point of view though, certainly coming about in modernity, sees Lilith as going rogue in response to an unreasonable husband who demands the dominant position in sexual intercourse and in making her argument that she was created from the same dust of the ground as Adam and thereby was worthy of equality. Lilith, unlike Eve in the creation account of Gen 2, was not formed from the body of the man, and therefore must not be subservient to him.

Now, in regards to the "Zohar," that other late medieval Jewish writing that has something a bit more substantial to say about Lilith; this work dates to around 1200 CE. It consists of twenty two total volumes and was written by rabbi Moses de Leon of Spain, although legend states that it was written back in the second century CE by a Jew hiding in a cave from the Roman army. It has sense been determined that this legend was a creation of Moses de Leon, who while writing under a penname, sought to give the work a special divine feel and ancient authority. The word "Zohar" means "enlightenment," or "brightness/splendor." It is highly regarded amongst the works of the Jewish mystic sect known as Kabbalah and is even considered its most important literary work, having also been the result of a long oral tradition.

There are some sixty direct and indirect references to Lilith in the Zohar. These support all the fundamental elements of the Lilith legend that have been passed down from the oral tradition and literary references that we have discussed in the previous pages. Basically, she is created at the same time as Adam from the dust of the earth, then became an unsuitable helpmate, fled from him, and finally became the tempting serpent and one with Samael (i.e. Satan). There are four passages in the Zohar in which Lilith is extensively drawn upon. We cite portions of these in the paragraph to follow.

For starters, we refer to what is known as Zohar I, 19b, which supports the Lilith legend that she abandoned Adam and became a murderer of children. Like much of the Zohar, the passage is cryptic and difficult to follow for those who are especially not familiar with Kabbalistic works. Small portions of the passage read, "When she saw Eve . . . she flew from there," and "she flees and goes through the world, finding infants who ought to be punished, and she smiles at them and kills them." It is rabbinic footnotes and commentary that elaborates on the "she" in the passage being identified with Lilith as one who intended to associate with Adam and have intercourse with him for the purpose of creating demon offspring but she was deterred by the beauty of Eve. In a second passage of the Zohar (Zohar I, 148a-148b), like the first passage, Lilith is not explicitly named, but is nonetheless strongly supported in the tradition as being her and being associated with the snake and the female of Samael. This nameless Lilith is beautiful, seductive, and a killer of men. Lilith does get mentioned by name in Zohar III, 19a. In this third of the four most important passages of the Zohar regarding Lilith she is the first wife of Adam in the creation story. We provide small selections of the passage where she is mentioned by name. For instance, at the beginning of the passage it states, "Come and see. From the crevice of the great deep, above, there came a certain female, the spirit of all spirits, and we have already explained that her name was Lilith. And at the very beginning she existed with man." Or later on, when it states, "When Lilith saw this she fled, and she is now in the cities of the sea, and she is still intent on injuring mankind." It even provides an explanation of Isa 34:14 and a future judgment upon Lilith when it states, "He will bring up Lilith and settle her in the ruins, because it will be desolate forever. This is the meaning of Lilith shall repose there, and find her place of rest." Lastly, a fourth passage from the Zohar regarding Lilith, Zohar III, 76b-77a, mentions Lilith by name one time, "They all go to Lilith first and she rears them. She goes out into the world in search of babies, and when she sees human babies she attaches herself to them, seeking to kill them, and to absorb the spirits of these human babies." The passage is really more about

Eve and her supposed sexual relationship with the snake to sire Cain than it is Lilith, but where Lilith is concerned it teaches her malevolence toward infants and warns that men be holy during intercourse lest Lilith take his child when it is born. In sum, Lilith appears in the Zohar in all of her guises: a contemporary with Adam who becomes an estranged seducer of other men, a serpent-like temptress, and procreator of demon offspring while seeking to do harm to human offspring.

SUMMARY

To review our study of Lilith then, we know that the proper noun "Lilith" appears in only one place in the Bible, Isaiah 34:14, although some have tried to see her in-between the lines of Gen 1-5. This sole biblical reference to Lilith is contained within a larger section of judgment texts in Isaiah with the nation of Edom being in particular focus. Lilith keeps company in the surrounding verses with frightful desert creatures such as jackals, ostriches, owls, wolves, goats, hawks, and snakes. For this reason, Lilith is often associated with being a night animal or some sort of nocturnal monster that is a rather allusive and mysterious being or creature. English translations verify this, although some translations keep the actual word "Lilith" in the text.

It seems that this minimal use of the term in the Bible is due to its non-Israelite origins. The Lilith legend is likely to have grown in ancient Babylonian or larger Mesopotamian mythology, but this is not entirely clear, as Lilith can be found in other ancient cultures as well. Even so, some scholars would contend for a non-mythological interpretation of Lilith, allowing the term to simply refer to a literal animal of some sort. Some twentieth century scholarly discussions concerning the identity of Lilith revolved around Sumerian and Syrian evidences by which some scholars made connections with the biblical Lilith. Other scholars refuted the evidence.

Isaiah's use of the term appears to be for the purpose of capturing the imaginations of the Israelite people who would have understood the terror that the idea of Lilith could bring. Lilith's origins in Mesopotamian culture and folklore show her to quite possibly be much more than a bird-like animal. Instead, Lilith might have been understood to be a female demon, or even a group of female demons, that fly around seducing and killing single men and devouring infants and ruining pregnancies.

Whereas Lilith is hardly mentioned in the Bible, she has much greater significance in later Jewish literature. There is for instance in an early common era apocryphal work known as The Testament of Solomon a story of Lilith being stripped of her demonic power and hanged for all to see by Solomon. In the Talmud there are five incidental references to Lilith that occur during the discussion of other topics. But this is significant, in that it demonstrates that Lilith was at this time a well-known figure that needed no explanation. The Targum known as Pseudo-Jonathan adds a prayer to Aaron's famous Num 6:24-26 blessing that seems to have the Lilith legend in mind. By the late medieval period she plays a surprisingly large role in the Zohar, a Kabalistic Midrash of Jewish mysticism.

It seems however that much of the Lilith legend developed from a rather spurious medieval work entitled The Alphabet of Ben Sira; where Lilith took on the role of being Adam's first wife, prior to Eve, who basically went rogue because she demanded the dominant sexual position in intercourse, a posture that was disagreeable to Adam. She argued that she was created from the same dust of the ground as Adam and therefore was worthy of equality. Her and her husband fought often, and this led her on a mission to abandon Adam, and then to go on to eventually ruin the hopes and joys of early motherhood or expectant mothers by stealing or destroying children. According to the legend, after having had enough of Adam, she grew wings and flew away. God then commanded three angels to fetch her and return her to her husband, but only to the effect of a somewhat failed negotiation. The medieval rabbis may have enlarged this Lilith tradition so as to account for the two creation stories in Genesis. In Gen 1, Lilith was first created, and in Gen 2, Eve was then created from the rib of Adam so as to be the more submissive wife that did not characterize Lilith.

Archaeological digs have unearthed amulets and incantation bowls containing some early inscriptions about Lilith. However, Lilith has continued for a long time since antiquity to be popular in the imaginations of poets, sages, writers, artists and more.[7] For instance, the famed Renaissance painter Michelangelo, taking his cue from the medieval literature, depicted Lilith as a half-woman, half-snake creature perched on the Tree of Knowledge of Good and Evil, thereby bringing her into association with the seduction of humans in the Garden of Eden. Lilith's influence has even reached into the modern age, having become for some a symbol of power and freedom for various feminist movements that might tend to view her more as goddess rather than demon. This feminist view contends that male authors might have indeed created the legend of Lilith to serve as an antithesis to Eve, who represents a more docile partner to the male, one concerned with being a begetter and nurturer of children.[8] Erica Jong wrote a book in 1973 entitled "Fear of Flying" which sparked Jewish female responses to oppressive husbands who demand abusive, patriarchal marriages that kept women trapped.[9] The story of the winged Lilith and her flight from Adam is used to serve as a positive role model of oppressed wives not fearing flying away as Lilith had supposedly done from Adam. In fact, there is an abundance of Jewish feminist literature on the topic. "Lilith" even became the name of a Jewish feminist magazine founded in 1976 and "Lilith Fair" was the chosen name for an all-female concert tour and travelling music festival founded by Canadian musician Sarah Mclachlan from 1997-1999 and revived for a moment in 2010. This was a celebration of women in music using the mythological and independent Lilith as somewhat of a mascot for the endeavor. These are just a few examples of the fame of Lilith. Also, despite Lilith's one appearance with surety in biblical literature, we have stated that there has been some tendency to see evidences of her in other places in the Bible as well, particularly in early Genesis, and thus her reputation has grown disproportionately.[10] However, all post-biblical legends of Lilith have little to do with her meaning in Isaiah 34:14, which is certainly reflective of Mesopotamian mythology to one degree or another.

NOTES

1. Seitz, *Isaiah 1-39*, pp.237-238.

2. John D. W. Watts, *Isaiah 34-66 (Word Biblical Commentary)* (Waco, Tx.: Word Books, 1987), p.13.

3. Ibid., p.14.

4. In the early 20th century, S.N. Kramer argued for Ancient Near Eastern evidences of Lilith to be associated with the biblical Lilith. S.N. Kramer, *Gilgamesh and the Huluppu Tree: A Reconstructed Sumerian Text.* Assyriological Studies 10. Chicago, 1938, p.5. Other scholars refuted the evidence. See D. Opitz, Ausgrabungen und Forschungsreisen: Ur. *Archive für Orientforschung 8,* Graz, 1932, p.330; T.H. Gaster, A Canaanite Magical Text. *Orientalia 11,* 1942, pp.44, 50; H. Torczyner, A Hebrew Incantation against Night-Demons from Biblical Times. *Journal of Near Eastern Studies 6,* Chicago, 1947, p.29; and S. Ribichini, Lilith nell-albero Huluppu. *Atti del 1 Convego Italiano sul Vicino Oriente Antico.* Rome, 1976, pp.31-33.

5. David Stern and Mark J. Mirsky, *Rabbinic Fantasies: Imaginative Narratives from Classical Hebrew Literature* (New Haven, CT: Yale University Press, 1990), p.167.

6. Geoffrey W. Dennis, *The Encyclopedia of Jewish Myth, Magic, and Mysticism*, 2nd edition (Woodbury, MN: Llewellyn, 2007), p.273.

7. Barbara Black Koltuv, *The Book of Lilith* (York Beach, ME: Nicolas – Hays, 1986), pp.126-127.

8. Barbara Geller Nathanson, *"Lilith"* in the Oxford Companion to the Bible (New York: Oxford University Press, 1993), p.437.

9. Erica Jong, *Fear of Flying* (New York: Holt, 1973).

10. H. Wildberger, "Der Monotheismus Deuterojesajas" in Beiträge zur Alttestamentlichen Theologie (Göttingen: Vandenhoeck & Ruprecht, 1977), pp.506-530.

Conclusion

The famed Swiss Reformed theologian, Karl Barth, wrote a classic book entitled *The Word of God and the Word of Man* where he repeatedly spoke of the Bible's "strange new world."[1] We have contended in this book that the bible is indeed a world of the strange and mysterious when it comes to the variety of creatures that are presented in its texts. These often times serve as images of good versus evil, or order versus chaos. We have noted how the earliest human origin stories from Mesopotamia speak of ravaging monsters and beasts, which have continued to be a part of the landscape of human history and culture, even beyond the western enlightenment and into the present modern and postmodern periods. Such myth making, imagination, fabrication, and creativity have been ways for humans to deal with the harshest realities of life while seeking meaning in life and struggling to deal with fears of those things which are seen and those things which are unseen. Flat and narrowly myopic literal readings of the bible that at times lacks for imagination and creative insight to the bible's occasional and amazingly metaphorical maze fall far short of what is needed to appreciate the full depth of the biblical world's imagery. We therefore in this work have explored the meaning of the bible's mysterious creatures with an emphasis on three creatures that all appear in the book of the prophet Isaiah: Lucifer (Isa 14:12), Leviathan (Isa 27:1), and Lilith (Isa 34:14).

Lucifer appears in the bible only in the Isa 14:12 passage, and even at that the term "Lucifer" is a Latin translation of a Hebrew word. The term is most likely to be associated with the astral myths of the Ancient Near East with reference to Venus, the brightest luminary in the night sky that fades away as the daylight appears. This Isaiah text is contained within a judgment oracle against a king of Babylon who sees himself as the "brightest star in the sky" so to speak. The meaning of the text then, is to claim that such pride and arrogance may dominate the stage momentarily, but ultimately will give way to the glory of God, since Lucifer falls from heaven. Lucifer means "morning star," and as such is generally a positive term, as for instance in the modern day movement of "Luciferianism," which refers to a worldview of a group of people who see themselves as enlightened. A text similar to Isa 14:12 is Ezek 28:12-19, another oracle against a king of a foreign nation, this time, the king of Tyre. Similarly to Isa 14, this king is also cast out from a position of great honor and prestige. Such casting out was linked by the Fathers, although not the Reformers of the Christian Church, to Luke 10:18 and Rev 12:8-9, passages which clearly point to Satan as the fallen being. Eventually Lucifer became the proper name of Satan, which in the Old Testament simply means "adversary." Satan makes just a few Old Testament cameo appearances as an adversary in places like Zech 3:1 and Job 1-2, where he seems to be some sort of lieutenant to God, but in 1 Chron 21:1 he is acting alone and may be going for the first time by the proper name "Satan." By the intertestamental period other Satan-like beings appear and go by other names, such as "Mastema" in the book of Jubilees where he is the cause of evil. Such explanations of the concept of evil originating in one being is common in many cultures of the world, as it is in biblical culture.

By the time of the New Testament the person of Satan is clearly identified as the devil as well. In the Gospels, the devil, besides being Jesus' direct nemesis, can appear in the form of human agents and in the conflict between Jesus and Jewish religious leaders. In Paul's writings, the devil wears many hats; he buffets, thwarts, hinders, schemes, punishes, and tempts; and as such is more the picture of Satan that is known in popular Christianity today, a view that is not always consistent with the original biblical biography of Satan. The apocalyptic devil is the culmination of everything known of him in the bible as Rev 12:9 describes him not just as Satan and the devil, but as the dragon and serpent of old. The story of the devil then by the last book of the bible is that he originally may have had access to God such as in the book of Job, but eventually is thrown down out of heaven to the earth, then thrown down to the abyss, and then finally thrown into the lake of fire. In fact, according to Luke 10:18, the devil may experience a fall everytime the Gospel is preached.

Besides the devil, aka "Lucifer," falling, there is within the biblical world the mystery of other fallen angels as well as demons and beings opposed to God being present. For example, the bible, especially in the writings of Paul, speaks of allusive entities knows as "principalities, powers, rulers, authorities, dominions, and thrones." They never receive any definition but appear to be both natural and supernatural powers that are aligned with darkness but are defeated ultimately by Christ's kingdom. Conversely, there are heavenly creatures and angels such as cherubim and seraphim which protect and advance Christ's cause. But as far as the devil goes, his title as "Lucifer" may have been blown out of proportion in popular interpretation, but there can be little doubt that his role as Satan the adversary grows and develops across the span of the bible.

Leviathan is another mysterious creature found in the book of Isaiah, 27:1 to be specific, and is also found in a few other places in the Old Testament. This dragon-like monster of the sea represented danger and deception. An associated creature, the snake, was actually deified in ancient cultures because of fear for this animal, whereas in the bible serpents can be conquered and become non-harmful, and sea monsters can give praise to God. But the sea monster motif in the bible is less about literal creatures and more about malevolent human dictators, associated empires, and evil in general, which can be found everywhere; for the serpent can coil itself on the land, raise itself in the air, and swim in the sea, thereby existing in land, air, and sea. However, in the bible, Leviathan is tamed by God and his place to swim, the sea, is eliminated in the apocalypse, thus indicating the eradication of evil. There are suggested naturalistic interpretations of Leviathan, and for that matter, her land colleague, Behemoth, but these must give way to the larger concern of supernatural interpretation. These creatures really belong to two worlds, one from the natural animal kingdom, and one from the world of the spiritual, mysterious, and even mythical. Leviathan and Behemoth are analogous to suffering and evil in the world and indicate how difficult it is to grasp such concepts because they are mysterious and allusive. Leviathan at times goes by the name Rahab as well in the Old Testament, but this appears to be used as a term specifically for the power of the nation of Egypt.

The rise of apocalyptic literature certainly further introduced the strange, bizarre, and mysterious to the theological thought world of the bible. Ezekiel's visions of the throne of God with associated living beings/Cherubim and Isaiah's only time mentioning of the Seraphim in the bible reveal that there are larger cosmic forces at work in the world. These forces will indeed break into the human sphere, as is the case with Daniel's vision of a stone that gets cut out of a mountain without human hands to destroy the statue in Nebuchadnezzar's dream which was representative of human kingdoms. In other words, God breaks in from the spiritual plane to correct the errors and evils of human power brokers. There is a similar situation when the same king Nebuchadnezzar has a second dream, that of a large tree being chopped down by a supernatural being, thereby reiterating the same point, that God's kingdom will defeat the kingdom of evil. In the book of Daniel archangels and spiritual princes are involved in a cosmic fight and earthly kingdoms are represented by natural beasts such as lions, leopards, bears, and indescribable terrifying beasts. In the New Testament apocalypse, the book of Revelation, Satan, also referred to as a dragon, serpent, and the devil of old, takes a leading role against God in the cosmic campaign. The "open door" of Rev 4:1 is an invitation to enter into the apocalyptic and heavenly realm of where God dwells on his throne along with the lamb that is the lion, ruling over creation and defeating the forces of evil in the cosmos. All kinds of mysterious creatures and beings are revealed in this heavenly show room. There are the four horses and horseman of the apocalypse and creatures from the abyss just to name a few. Yet the many plagues and judgments in Revelation are reminiscent of what took place in Egypt against the Pharaoh of long ago. History in a sense repeats itself, and the point is that human leaders rise up in arrogance against God but ultimately end up defeated by him. This involves both the past and the present, with a particular eye on the Roman empire of John's day when writing the last book of the Christian biblical canon. And although strange and mysterious creatures feature in the biblical landscape, the primary concern is always for God, his rule over the earth, and the place for his people in his reign. As concerns Leviathan, by the end of the canon there is no place for him to swim anymore as the sea (chaos and disorder) has been eliminated (Rev 21:1). The apocalyptic destruction of the dragon spells the end for Leviathan and his minions and removes all external threats to God's kingdom.

The third and final mysterious creature that we have explored in this work is Lilith, who appears in the bible only in Isa 34:14. Because of this, Lilith is fairly unknown in the religious world but is surprisingly more known in the secular world. The one scant reference to her in the bible places her amongst haunting desert creatures in an oracle of judgment against the nation of Edom. However, outside the bible, Lilith became known as Adam's first wife, prior to Eve, who became rebellious and a terrorizer of little children and pregnant women. The first known reference to her in extra-biblical literature comes from as far back as 2000 BCE in a work called *Gilgamesh and the Huluppu Tree*, which is part of the famed *Gilgamesh Epic*. In this story, Lilith, who is clearly an ene-my, is driven away from the coveted tree by the hero Gilgamesh. There are other Mesopotamian artifacts which bear witness to the Lilith legend as well, such as the Burney relief, a clay artifact that arguably portrays in its art work Lilith as the central figure. Also, the Nippur bowls, which served for the purposes of incantation, featured Lilith in the task of warding off demons and diseases. Even the more sophisticated Talmud preserved the Lilith legend. The *Testament of Solomon*, placed between 200-600 CE reveals a Lilith with long hair who is put to death for her basic witchery. There is a sneak peak of Lilith in the Aramaic Targum known as *Pseudo Jonathan*, whereas there is a much more sustained treat-ment of Lilith in the *Alphabet of Ben Sira*, which dates to about 800-900 CE. This is an incredibly irreverent work which also pro-vides an explanation for the two creation accounts in Genesis, whereby Lilith and Eve both supposedly feature as the wives of Adam. There are also significant Kabbalistic works which feature Lilith, such as the 1100 CE *Book of Raziel* which speaks of Lilith the child slayer as a "primitive Eve." A slightly later Kabbalistic work, the *Zohar*, has four or so passages that draw extensively upon Lilith.

To a certain extent, Lilith has grown into a movement in the modern day. Her role as villain is replaced as heroine who stands up against dictatorial husbands and any bigoted patriarchy that at-tempts to keep femininity at bay. Thus, these mysterious creatures of the bible live on and can both inspire and cause fear. It is a marvelous mixed world of biblical metaphor and realism to be found in the likes of Lucifer, Leviathan, Lilith and the rest of the mysterious creatures that make a biblical appearance. Reader imagination and appreciation for creativity is necessary when crossing into the world of the ancients who gave us the bible and who are reminding us of a much larger world that is not so visible to the human eye, where faith is expected as well. Humans live with daily struggles and deep underlying fears that are a part of the human psyche, as is evidenced by superstitions that have stretched from early times into modern times. The universal and continual appeal of the dragon for instance, and the popularity of the monster business in the current United States to be seen every October and by taking a cursory glance at the movie section of libraries reinforce this notion. In a word, the mysterious creatures of the bible help us humans to properly place ourselves in both the natural and supernatural worlds where good and evil, and order and chaos are at war with one another, and where the kingdom of God, so clearly expressed in the bible, has the final say and gains the final victory over all disorder.

NOTE

1. Karl Barth, *The Word of God and the Word of Man* (Gloucester, ME: Peter Smith Publishers, 1928).

Bibliography

Armstrong, Karen. *A Short History of Myth*. Edinburgh, New York, Melbourne: Canongate, 2005.

Baldwin, Joyce G. *Daniel: An Introduction & Commentary*. Tyndale Old Testament Commentaries. Edited by D.J. Wiseman. Downers Grove: InterVarsity Press, 1978.

Barth, Karl. *The Word of God and the Word of Man*. Gloucester: Peter Smith Publishers, 1928.

Berlin, Adele and Marc Zvi Brettler. *The Jewish Study Bible Tanakh Translation*. Oxford, New York: Oxford University Press, 2004.

Brownlee, William H. *Ezekiel 1-19*. Word Biblical Commentary. Waco: Word Books, 1986.

Clements, Ronald E. *Isaiah 1-39*. The New Century Bible Commentary. Grand Rapids: William B. Eerdmans Publishing Company, 1980.

Danker, Frederick William. *A Greek-English Lexicon of the New Testament and other Early Christian Literature* (3rd edition, BDAG). Chicago, London: The University of Chicago Press, 2000.

Davis, Kenneth C. *Don't Know Much About Mythology*. New York: Harper Collins Publishers, 2005.

Dennis, Geoffrey W. *The Encyclopedia of Jewish Myth, Magic, and Mysticism*, 2nd edition Woodbury, MN: Llewellyn, 2007.

De Young, Donald B. *Dinosaurs and Creation: Questions and Answers*. Grand Rapids: Baker Books, 2000.

Duling, D.C. *Testament of Solomon (The Old Testament Pseudepigrapha, volume 1)*. Edited by James H. Charlesworth. New York: Doubleday, 1983.

Eliot, Alexander. *The Global Myths: Exploring Primitive, Pagan, Sacred, and Scientific Mythologies*. New York: The Continuum Publishing Company, 1993.

Ford, Michael W. *Beginning Luciferian Magick*. Houston, TX: Succubus Productions, 2008.

Fyall, Robert S. *Now my Eyes have seen You: Images of creation and evil in the book of Job*. New Studies in Biblical Theology. Edited by D.A. Carson. Downers Grove: InterVarsity Press, 2002.

Gaster, T.H. A Canaanite Magical Text. *Orientalia 11*, 1942.

Goldingay, John. *The Theology of the Book of Isaiah*. Downers Grove: IVP Academic, 2014.

Gray, George B. *Isaiah I-XXVII* (The International Critical Commentary). Edinburgh: T&T Clark, 1975.

Grenz, Stanley J., and David Guretzki and Cherith Fee Nordling. *Pocket Dictionary of Theological Terms*. Downers Grove: InterVarsity Press, 1999.

Grogan, Geoffrey W. *Isaiah* (The Expositor's Bible Commentary, vol.6). Edited by Frank E. Gaebelein. Grand Rapids: Zondervan, 1986.

Hall, Angus. *Monsters and Mythic Beasts*. Garden City: Doubleday and Company Inc., 1976.

Isaac, E. *1 Enoch (The Old Testament Pseudepigrapah, vol.1)*. Edited by James H. Charlesworth. New York: Doubleday, 1983.

Jong, Erica. *Fear of Flying*. New York: Holt, 1973.

Kelly, Henry Ansgar. *Satan: A Biography*. Cambridge: Cambridge University Press, 2006.

Klein, Ralph W. *Ezekiel: The Prophet and His Message*. Columbia: University of South Carolina Press, 1988.

Koltuv, Barbara Black. *The Book of Lilith*. York Beach: Nicolas – Hays, 1986.

Kramer, S.N. *Gilgamesh and the Huluppu Tree: A Reconstructed Sumerian Text*. Assyriological Studies 10. Chicago, 1938.

Leeming, David Adams. *The World of Myth: an Anthology*. New York, Oxford: Oxford University Press, 1990.

Lockyer, Herbert. *Satan: His Person & Power*. Waco: Word Books, 1980.

Lunt, H.G. *The Apocalypse of Abraham (The Old Testament Pseudepigrapha, vol.1)*. Edited by James H. Charlesworth. New York: Doubleday, 1983.

Morris, Leon. *Revelation* (Tyndale New Testament Commentaries, Revised Edition). Leicester: InterVarsity Press, 1992.

Nathanson, Barbara Geller. *"Lilith"* in the Oxford Companion to the Bible. New York: Oxford University Press, 1993.

Noll, Stephen F. *Angels of Light, Powers of Darkness: Thinking Biblically About Angels, Satan & Principalities*. Downers Grove: InterVarsity Press, 1998.

Opitz, D. Ausgrabungen und Forschungsreisen: Ur. *Archive für Orientforschung 8*, Graz, 1932.

Osborn, Kevinand Dana L. Burgess. *Classical Mythology: the Complete Idiot's Guide*. New York: Alpha Books, 1998.

Oswalt, John. *The Book of Isaiah Chapters 1-39* (The New International Commentary on the Old Testament). Grand Rapids: William B. Eerdmans Publishing Company, 1986.

Pagels, Elaine. *The Origin of Satan*. New York: Random House Inc., 1995.

Payne, J. Barton. *1, 2 Chronicles* (The Expositor's Bible Commentary). Edited by Frank E. Gaebelein. Grand Rapids: Zondervan, 1988.

Priest, J. *Testament of Moses (The Old Testament Pseudepigrapha, vol.1)*. Edited by James H. Charlesworth. New York: Doubleday, 1983.

Rienecker, Fritzand Cleon Rogers. *Linguistic Key to the Greek New Testament*. Grand Rapids: Zondervan Publishing House, 1976.

Ribichini, S. Lilith nell-albero Huluppu. *Atti del 1 Convego Italiano sul Vicino Oriente Antico*. Rome, 1976.

Russell, Jeffery Burton. *The Prince of Darkness: Radical Evil and the Power of Good in History*. Ithaca and London: Cornell University Press, 1988.

Seitz, Christopher R. *Isaiah 1-39* (Interpretation: A Bible Commentary for Teaching and Preaching). Louisville: John Knox Press, 1993.

Smick, Elmer B. *Job* (The Expositor's Bible Commentary, vol.4). Edited by Frank E. Gaebelein. Grand Rapids: Zondervan, 1988.

South, Malcolm. *Mythical and Fabulous Creatures: A Sourcebook and Research Guide*. New York: Peter Bedrick Books, 1987.

Stern, David and Mark J. Mirsky, *Rabbinic Fantasies: Imaginative Narratives from Classical Hebrew Literature*. New Haven, CT: Yale University Press, 1990.

Torczyner, H. A Hebrew Incantation against Night-Demons from Biblical Times. *Journal of Near Eastern Studies 6*, Chicago, 1947.

Twelftree, G.H. *New Dictionary of Biblical Theology*. Leicester and Downers Grove: InterVarsity Press, 2000.

Walton, J.H. *Dictionary of the Old Testament Pentateuch*. Edited by T. Desmond Alexander and David W. Baker. Downers Grove. Leicester: InterVarsity Press, 2003.

Walton, John H. *The Lost World of Genesis One*. Downers Grove: InterVarsity Press, 2009.

Watts, John D.W. *Isaiah 1-33* (Word Biblical Commentary). Waco: Word Books, 1985.

Watts, John D.W. *Isaiah 34-66* (Word Biblical Commentary). Waco: Word Books, 1987.

Wildberger, H. "Der Monotheismus Deuterojesajas" in *Beiträge zur Alttestamentlichen Theologie*. Göttingen: Vandenhoeck & Ruprecht, 1977.

Wilkings, Ernest Hatch and Thomas Goddard Bergin. *A Concordance to the Divine Comedy of Dante Alighieri*. Cambridge: The Belknap Press of Harvard University Press, 1965.

Wintermute, O.S. *Jubilees (The Old Testament Pseudepigrapha, vol.1)*. Edited by James H. Charlesworth. New York: Doubleday, 1985.

Wray, T.J. and Gregory Mobley. *The Birth of Satan: Tracing the Devil's Biblical Roots*. New York: Palgrave Macmillan, 2005.

Youngblood, Ronald F. *1, 2 Samuel* (The Expositor's Bible Commentary, vol.3). Edited by Frank E. Gaebelein. Grand Rapids: Zondervan, 1992.

CPSIA information can be obtained
at www.ICGtesting.com
Printed in the USA
LVHW090145180821
695561LV00003B/56